SOUTH JERSEY
LEGENDS & LORE

SOUTH JERSEY LEGENDS & LORE

TALES FROM THE PINE BARRENS AND BEYOND

WILLIAM J. LEWIS

THE
History
PRESS

Published by The History Press
Charleston, SC
www.historypress.com

First published 2024

Manufactured in the United States

ISBN 9781467156370

Library of Congress Control Number: 2023949149

Way back when this author was still at Allentown High School in New Jersey, an English teacher taught him it was OK to write for pleasure—that not all things need be driven in terms of dollars made. I am forever thankful for that life lesson. This book of stories is dedicated to you, Mrs. Kris Olsen, my creative writing teacher!

CONTENTS

ILLUSTRATIONS

FOREWORD

William Lewis has been and continues to be a great inspiration for his fellow advocates in bringing back the culture and love of the life of a Piney. I was brought into this journey early on in his writing career, where, at the time, he was in search of a graphic designer to help spread awareness of his work. One opportunity led to another, and eventually our relationship blossomed into an author/illustrator partnership for a single young adult (YA) book. If not for that project, I would not be where I am today. I am studying fine arts at the College of New Jersey, working during the summer to promote art inspired by the stories of visiting authors on campus. My uncle, who is one of the largest inspirations in my life, took a chance on a self-taught artist and gave me the outlet and confidence I needed to decide to pursue my dreams as a professional artist.

For all my life, these are the traits I have come to associate with the character of my uncle. I remember in particular the Christmases of my childhood, when he would host wreath-making events using locally harvested grapevine he had handpicked himself—giving back to the community in a way that encouraged an appreciation for the natural beauty of the Pines and the great outdoors. The natural beauty of these Pineycrafts would warm the hearts of strangers, bringing smiles to boys and girls excited to participate in the holiday tradition.

Lewis's commitment to the Pines extends far beyond a personal hobby. He lives and breathes the ecosystem and what flourishes within it, keeping a personal blog full of photographed flora and detailing his research and personal experiences growing up in a family of Piney ancestry.

While working on this book as its illustrator, I had the chance to interpret each story and retell them through charcoal. Charcoal as the medium of choice grants the artist the ability to freeze a moment in time, while its variations of black and white help ground it in realism. Few stories manage to seamlessly bring the reader into another world, but the evident emotions and personal touch through each account make it feel as if you are just as allured by the Pine Barrens' pull as the characters within this book. It was an honor to pay homage to those feelings in the paintings throughout, and it was a thrilling experience to funnel in my own feelings at the end of each reading. These individual tales come together in a way that shares the story of one character, the Pine Barrens. It is the thread that has united thousands of New Jerseyans over the generations, and it continues to create and inspire new stories deep in its sea of green.

Shane Tomalinas
Allentown, New Jersey

PREFACE

G et on the stagecoach of old and take a ride with us through hundreds of years of history and one thousand miles crisscrossing southern New Jersey. These pages add up to chapters and finally a book, holding a collection of thirty different fables, myths, lore and historical tales of yore, running the gamut of topics with one central green thread, the New Jersey Pine Barrens. This writer does not always want to write what the reader wants to read, especially if you're a local historian in a state that was once divided by a province line, creating two provinces: East and West. John Adams, even after the state became one, called us the Jerseys. And in New Jersey, West Jersey mainly resides in southern New Jersey and has as many quirky tall tales as Greek mythology. So, it's even harder for a Pine Barrens historian such as yours truly to avoid the myths and legends that have grown to exponential proportions—taller even than the beanstalk Jack climbed up. They're especially hard to ignore when the state itself promotes southern New Jersey's most famous cryptid, the Jersey Devil, at every turn. One can't outrun the fright.

What's a writer to do when, time and again, a story or a theme bursts out and continues to grow, as if it grew legs of its own? Why, they would do what any smart businessperson would do: catch the critter and sell it. Give the people what they want to read. Legendary stories alongside historical old-time history of provenance of both places and people that lend credence to the popular myths and fables. This book has got it all: romance, mystery, history and a devil or two. And where it debunks one or two legends, it births another three or four. The acts of pirates Captain Kidd and Blackbeard are children's tales compared to the picarooning of the real-life Pine Robbers of legend. We hope these old and even taller tales are told in a way that will continue the merriment of storytelling around a campfire. And I also hope that local history as told by the historian once and for all proves that fact is stranger than fiction nearly 99 percent of the time. The common people doing extraordinary things sometimes get lost among the recorded volumes of the historical deeds of George Washington, who traipsed across the state of New Jersey and boated across the Delaware River into Trenton. In this book, I focus on old-time stories that prove there are lessons to be learned from history and that local history still has some fight left in it. Yet in other chapters, I capture some of those squirrelly tales that can be read by the light of a campfire, adding to the scare and fright of the night. You've been warned.

Legal disclaimer: Unless otherwise indicated, all the names, characters, businesses, places, events and incidents in this book are either the product of the author's imagination, myth or fable, and are used in a fictitious manner. Any resemblance to actual persons—living or dead—or actual events is purely coincidental. I do not advise you to trespass or disobey any laws of the land. Again, parts of this work are based on real events. Certain events, dialogue and characters were created for the purposes of fictionalization.

ACKNOWLEDGEMENTS

Oral history, to this author, is as important—if not more important—than any other historical factoid in this world. Storytelling is a way for one generation to pass the knowledge of the past to the next, who can then carry forward the lessons of yesterday into the future. When a link in the chain breaks, we lose vast volumes of knowledge. Whether the participants in the preparation of this book provided folklore or historical fact, I thank them. Without the dozens of individuals who contributed their stories, this book would not be possible. And it is in our hearts and hopes that we aid that custodial chain of our collective history to be forever intact. Those who contributed a story or family fable know who they are, and I thank them for sharing their knowledge with me, thus becoming part of the struggle to continue the traditions and culture of yesteryear.

I would especially like to thank my mother, Charlotte Lewis, and father, Joseph Lewis, who embraced storytelling as a way of life. To my nephew Shane Tomalinas, who wrote the foreword and was the illustrator for this project, I say a big thank-you. To the keepers of family history, we owe a debt of gratitude: Clare Nurko, Thelma Davison, Mrs. Gail Miller, Mrs. Rose Marshall, Mrs. MaryEllen Rogers, Ms. Elizabeth Tumm and Mrs. Lois Danieski. Scores of others contributed to the monumental task of writing this book. A writer's inspiration comes from many wells. One of the biggest supporters of local history and lovers of South Jersey Online is the group known as Piney Tribe. I thank each and every one of you who cared enough to add your voice to the collective community in support of our writing and adventures.

1

WHY DOES THE DARK SCARE US SO?

It's 9:00 p.m. and there's a knock at the door, but you're home alone and the sudden tapping at the front door scares the bejesus out of you. All day long, someone can come to the front door and rap the knocker like an escaped lunatic and it wouldn't bother you as much as it does after the sun goes down. The same feeling occurs indoors if you let your imagination escape you. You wake in the middle of the night and see a shadow next to the window. It must be a person who may be a real-life boogie man coming to take you away. Things in your room take on funny shapes when the light is turned down, even though you've been in that room a million times and know each shape of the furniture like you know your own face—at least in the daytime. But the boogie man usually works the second shift, and everything that is scary comes out just as the sun sets.

Some will blame an overactive imagination for the haunting of our dark hours. Others will point to storytellers in our midst. Those who cast a tale where the punchline to a joke is murder and mayhem, which, to the overactive mind, is a potentially real outcome in the dark of night. We are told as children that all bad things happen when the lights are turned off. If you don't go to sleep, the boogie man under your bed will get you. Hansel and Gretel, with their father, ventured into the dark as if they didn't know bad things lurk in the Black Forest of Germany. These old fairy tales take on lives of their own, becoming more than stories to ward children away from bad behavior—tall tales indeed. Master storytellers continue the tradition of crafting scary tales that build on the old stories of the past and add new,

Stories of Childhood. *Artist, Shane Tomalinas.*

darker twists. And over time, a new generation becomes frighted from all that they already know to be true and what the mind fabricates as a new reality in the pitch black of night.

Those stories become real-life experiences in which you trust little of what you can't see with your own eyes. Even though you know the person at the front door is the expected delivery person bringing an online purchase and not someone there to deliver murder and mayhem to your life. And the ghost of a man next to your window—as if the boogie man would stand by the window and not right by your bed—is really a sweater you left out on a hanger to dry. The mind loves a good mystery, but the heart races in anticipation of what it could be and the fact that it could want to harm us. Our collective brains have been trained to sleep in the dark and play in the light. It works overtime in the night to bring us a fright. Next time you're around a child, remember we've found the source of all bad dreams and nightmares. It's the people among us who like to tell little children scary stories to make them behave. So, you have a choice to make. You can be the creator of the light or add another creature to the night.

2

THE ONCE HURLEY HOUSE OF JACKSON, NEW JERSEY FAME

Nowadays in the Pines, you are oft to see a wayward traveler heading down a sandy dirt road, seeking out a forgotten town. The notion of finding a lost town is somehow mysterious, romantic and exciting. But more than likely, the people who lived in that space long ago had harsh realities. Life was to live hand to mouth. Today's twenty-first-century conveniences have made our lives more comfortable, but electricity, running water, home heating and cooling—and, later, the internet—were lacking in many of the Piney homesteads until the 1960s. The images in this chapter are from a location that was once an important family homestead, a wellspring of life for the folks who raised their families there. We are now just a few generations removed from the naming of this corner at the edge of two busy townships in southern New Jersey. It was named for the Archer family, who came before the following tale took place. Archers Corner and its namesake are now forgotten, and the people who took up residence where the Archers once plowed fields are now disappearing, too. But let us embark on that tale so that remnants of their passing can still be seen and their stories can be told.

Our imaginations tend to fill in the blanks for us, painting a picture with bright, cheery colors, whereas many of the inhabitants of forgotten places would more than likely have used darker colors—maybe various shades and tones of black or gray. Every cloud did not have a silver lining; sometimes, it had more of a dark, ominous undertone. The stories of the poor are easily forgotten. Usually, their stories are never written down and printed in a

Left: Hurley House of Old.
Artist, Shane Tomalinas.

Below: Photograph by Joseph
P. Czarnecki, October 6, 1983.
*Pinelands Folklife Project collection
(AFC 1991/023), American
Folklife Center, Library of Congress.*

book, and they are never remembered for the work they did with little at hand and small parcels of land.

In 1983, by a stroke of sheer luck, this roadside vegetable stand captured the eye of photographer Joseph Czarnecki, who, at the time, was part of a team spearheaded by the American Folklife Center collaborating with several state and federal agencies documenting the folklife of the residents of the New Jersey Pinelands. Joseph Czarnecki was the main project photographer. It's unclear how an image of that roadside vegetable stand was selected as the cover photograph for the book *Pinelands Folklife*. To the locals, it is just a country farmstand like so many others littered across the highways of southern New Jersey, but it does give one a rare opportunity to peer into the poor farmer's window—to look back at their personal history, even though the farmstand and homestead they built are now gone. Often, their stories are forgotten—but not this time.

After contacting two members of the federally funded Pinelands Folklife Project, one can still only guess about why this image was chosen to represent the entire Pine Barrens culture. On April 13, 2020, *Burlington County Times* photojournalist Dennis McDonald, who also worked as a part-time photographer assigned to the Pinelands Folklife Center working directly for Mary Hufford, stated:

> *It's a good question about why Joseph Czarnecki's photo got selected as the cover, but I'm not aware of the reason. I guess they thought the farmstand, with its self-serve look as opposed to someone running one of those monster farmstands you see everywhere, was appealing. And the house behind it, with that washed cedar look, must have struck them as being typical of the area. The Pinelands Folklife Project was huge. It had a lot of people involved in it. It must have been someone's idea of what the Pinelands looked like to an outsider. I love the house like others in the Pines with that weathered look. The farmstand looks like one of the types where you leave the money in the box kind of place. The variety of vegetables and stuff is neat. Probably driven by it a million times—as other farm stands throughout South Jersey. If I am not in the buying mood, I just look at it and drive by. It is a classic look. It does say South Jersey but not specifically the Pines to me.*

The second person contacted to try to solve the mystery of why the image was chosen was Mary Hufford, the project's director based out of Washington, D.C. In an electronic correspondence, Mary said, "Regarding how the photo was chosen for the cover of Pinelands Folklife, I don't know how that was chosen. It was taken during the Pinelands Folklife Project and is a beautiful image. I have a blown-up version of that framed in my home." It remains a mystery why that image was chosen to represent the 1.1 million acres of the New Jersey Pinelands, but the owners of that home and their stories are captured here for the first time.

Let us revisit the image that photographer Joseph Czarnecki took back in 1983 and observe the story of the people who lived within the four sides of that snapshot. It should be noted that the home has since been demolished and removed from the landscape. The owner of the once dirt-floor house and eight-acre farm was William Edward Hurley Sr., whom everyone endearingly called Uncle Ed. Ed, with his wife, Margaret "Emery" Hurley, raised five of their children and Margaret's niece Cheryl. The children, in order from oldest to youngest, were named William Jr., Harry, Frank, Dixie and Zanetta. Behind those weathered and worn cedar-shingled walls, Ed and Margaret kept the home warmed with one wood stove, but their love wrapped around the family, enabling them to live happy lives. Uncle Ed was a thrifty person. He was so thrifty that his brother-in-law Joseph Emery used to say, "Ed's still got the first dollar he ever made." Joseph Emery farmed his four acres located to the south on Hawkins Road. Ed had twice the acreage of his brother-in-law situated on Veterans Highway. The two relied on each other quite a bit, pulling their resources and hands together when needed. Ed was old-school and lived frugally. When Ed died, the kids had to dig up the yard, as Ed kept all his money buried in glass jars. Like most of his generation, he didn't trust the banks—and for good reason.

Joseph Lewis, a family friend who also married into the family, said, "Ed had grown a special kind of pink variety of tomatoes, and he was smart and sharp, even into his later years in life." The tomatoes were called Pop's pinks. There is a pink tomato variety in seed catalogues today. Ed and Margaret also worked the land, growing other Jersey crops like sweet potatoes, eggplants, squash, beets and watermelons. Ed's bestsellers were baskets of cantaloupes and baskets of sweet potatoes. He also worked at the local Agway for twenty years in addition to working the roadside vegetable stand now famously pictured on the cover of *Pinelands Folklife*.

By the time the photograph of the stand was taken in 1983, most of the children had grown up and moved out—all but Ed's eldest son, Billy Hurley. Later on, Ed and Margaret both retired, and in 2005, when both were in their eighties, they, along with their son Billy, moved in with their son Frank Hurley at his home in New Egypt. Of note, Frank Hurley, like his

Above: William Edward Hurley Sr. at the homestead, 1366 West Veterans Highway, Jackson Township, New Jersey 08527. *Courtesy of the Hurley family.*

Right: Margaret "Emery" Hurley, wife of Ed Hurley. *Courtesy of the Hurley family.*

Opposite: *From left to right*: Joseph Emery, Frank Emery, Louis Joseph "Jack" Liptak and Ed Hurley, circa the 1940s. *Courtesy of the Hurley family.*

grandfather Charles Hurley, worked for the state and, at one time, lived in a house on the Colliers Mills Wildlife Management Area property. In the New Jersey Division of Fish and Wildlife, he was a renowned trapper. Ed and Margaret sold their home and land to a contractor. Their eight acres were zoned to contain four commercial acres and four residential acres. Whether the home's removal was the result of a real estate investment or another intention, the Hurley homestead fell into disrepair and was eventually torn down. Sadly, Ed passed away from cancer in 2005, but his wife, Margaret, lived to the ripe old age of ninety before passing away in 2014.

The earlier Hurley and Emery family trees take particularly strange turns as each branches out. If you trace the tree branches—and there were a lot of branches—and read the names of the wedded, you'll scratch your head at how many brothers and sisters are mixed up and married into the same family. The Hurleys, who owned that two-story farmhouse with a roadside veggie stand, for example, had: a set of brothers and sisters marry another set of brothers and sisters. Ed Hurley and Lavinia Hurley were siblings. Margaret Emery and Joseph Emery were siblings. William Edward Hurley Sr. married Margaret Emery, and Joseph Emery married Lavinia Hurley.

Looking back further through the window of the past, the Hurley clan got its start on East Colliers Mills Road in New Egypt. All that is left of Edward's boyhood home is a tree stump in the middle of the farm field that marks where the home once stood. Ed and his younger sister Lavinia moved to state property known as Colliers Mills WMA, where their father, Charles Andrew Hurley, managed the property for the state until they became adults. When Ed Hurley eventually married Margaret, the couple purchased farmland less than two miles north of Ed's father's house at 1366 West Veterans Highway, Jackson Township, New Jersey 08527. It's interesting to note that the families who lived on the eastern side of Hawkin Road were in Jackson Township, and those living across the street on the western side of Hawkin Road were in Plumsted Township.

Looking at the main tree trunk of the Hurley family conjures up more confusion. Charles Andrew Hurley and Lillian (previously Housekeeper) Hurley, after marrying and moving to New Egypt from Neptune, New Jersey, had a mess of children. Ed and Lavinia were just two of their children. Lillian (née Burroughs) from Trenton had two children from a previous marriage: Albert Housekeeper and Lillian Housekeeper. From oldest to youngest, Charles and Lillian were the parents of: Albert, Lillian, William "Uncle Ed," Jack, Lavinia, Genève, Bessie and Harold. Charles Hurley's brother John Hurley married the daughter of Charles's wife with the surname Housekeeper.

In the end, those large families of the past made the heavy load of daily life seem lighter. In mostly agrarian-based communities, these large families interacted with each other, often intermarrying. To be clear, families marrying into each other were not considered incestuous, but a pair of siblings marrying another pair of siblings with the same surname was. The crossroads of Hawkin Road and Veterans Highway (or Route 528) was the epicenter for the Emery and Hurley families starting in the mid-1900s. Ed and Margaret's home was located in Jackson, catty-corner the New Egypt–Jackson line. The New Egypt–Jackson line area is also the northern terminus of the New Jersey Pinelands National Reserve. A local resident and mason by the name of Christian "Chris" Villipart called himself and fellow New Egyptians "Edgers" (because they live on the edge of the New Jersey Pine Barrens). On the same Veteran's Highway, parallel and just down the road (about half a mile) from Ed and Margaret was their father Charles Hurley's brother Albert Hurley (uncle to Ed and Lavinia), who lived in Jackson but was closer to Cassville, once known as Goshen. There on the edge of the Pines, Ed Hurley's little sister lived just to the south, down Hawkin Road on the New Egypt side, and across the street from Lavinia was their uncle Arthur, who was a Jackson resident. And in between Ed's home on Veteran's Highway and Lavinia's home on Hawkin was the home of their uncle Frank "Paul" Emery, also on the Jackson

Right: Joseph Emery and William Edward Hurley Sr. repairing a Farmall tractor. *Courtesy of the Hurley family.*

Below: The north view of 1366 West Veterans Highway, November 2022. *Author's collection.*

The west view of 1366 West Veterans Highway, November 2022. *Author's collection.*

side. Oh, and I almost forgot—Joseph Emery's (Lavinia's husband's) sister Thelma owned a house and a trailer (part of New Egypt) located down Hawkin Road by the old horse track of Ephraim P. Emson, closer to the entrance of Colliers Mills WMA (part of New Egypt). Since then, the landscape has changed, and families have become spread out, but the history remains for those who know where to look.[1]

We dedicate this story to those who lived it. To all of Ed and Margaret's family, past and present, thank you. And I'd like to give an especially warm thank-you to Harry Hurley and Dianne Hurley, who helped tell their story. Also, a big thank-you to Lois Danieski, a part of the Hurley tree whom the author recently discovered is intertwined with the Housekeeper side of the family tree.

3

"DADDY, WHY DON'T YOU SAY I LOVE YOU?"

There's so much hurt in the world, but all we ever need is love to fix it. Love is a commodity traded at such volatile rates that it should be regulated and traded on the stock exchange in New York City. Some people trade it for nothing, while others make you pay a high price for just a pinch. Some don't ever exchange it, even though, from sitcom television shows, we learn families of all kinds gift it to each other. *Homo sapiens* may have the most complex and enduring vessel, yet it comes with the most fragile spirit. No one ever walks around and says, "My spirit animal is a Homo sapien!" We know from experience our world is cruel and built in such a fragile state and the market for love is manipulated to such a degree that it brings our species down. Invented love is crafted and sold in the guttered road as authentic, leaving us to only cry when we find out it's false.

Standing in the shadows of the late afternoon, there in the family's living room, a middle-aged woman says, "Daddy, why don't you say I love you? My life's been rough and a hell since I left these four walls behind. Now, years later, I return after finally learning what's ruined every relationship I've had in this cruel world. I made my way west without it and tumbled through town after town like a tumbleweed which I saw for the first time in my teens. With each slam of the door, I left behind a dirty man who reminded me of you. So much like you that he didn't say it either. They had names like Billy Bob, Jimmy, Rico, and even plain Joe. Maybe it's a certain type of man that doesn't dare to say it. It can't be courage though for after a few drinks I heard them all voice it, but they didn't mean it. All

House on Route 206, No More. *Artist, Shane Tomalinas.*

The house on Route 206 before it was demolished. *Jennifer Andzeski.*

they wanted was me in bed. And all I wanted was love and someone to sit with like I once did in this room here with you in your rickety rocking chair. Remember the last time I was here? I was only sixteen then and I told you I hated you and was tired of this cold old room and your cold old heart. That was the last time we saw each other and now I've grown old and cold just like you. Like father like daughter."

The broken-hearted woman then walked to the empty rocking chair in the center of the room and gave it a push.

Sadness comes from the depreciation of love in your life. Inflation can occur, too, but usually, it's not how the market of love works. Like the young woman rocking an empty chair, we value love whether it exists as a physical product or not. We'd pay inflated prices for it just to have a piece of happiness. And as life goes on, the phrase "life isn't fair" gets proven over and over. Some people don't realize they have experienced so much love in their lives that they could retire early and still ride out their lives happily. Meanwhile, others thirst for a taste of what others neglect and abuse, literally dying to be loved, traveling through life never feeling loved nor knowing how to love. We purchase things and lie with others, trying to fabricate what we covet so much, yet never achieving that authentic feeling that comes from a simple, heartfelt, "I love you." Bad decisions build up like a résumé after not being loved by a father or mother. But one day, the rocking chair rocks on its own and the story of a tormented life without love in it continues.[2]

4

ADVENTURES OF
THE KID BILLY

E very Wednesday, little Billy rides with his grandparents to the local flea
market. Spending the day with Grandma and Grandpa is way more
fun than being stuck with a babysitter. Mom and Dad are too busy to take
off work to even consider going to the flea market on a workday. They call it
hump day, but little Billy doesn't see it that way—he calls it the "bestest day
of the week!" He gets something to eat before he leaves and has lunch with
his grandparents while they are out at the flea market. There are hotdogs
and chips for everyone—it's a grand day. If you asked Billy how long he's
been coming to the New Egypt Flea Market Village, he'd tell you he's been
going all his life.[3] A boy all of seven years old doesn't have much experience
to measure things against. But as a typical little boy, curious and inquisitive,
Billy finds adventure down every row of the market. Today is no different.

Bright and early, Grandma and Grandpa pick up Billy from his parents'
house. With his favorite baseball hat on and a hug and kiss from Mom, he's
off to seek adventure among the rows of tables of old stuff on display and
older people to talk to. Mom and Dad seem like babies when Billy stops to
think about how old the people whom he sees hawking their wares at the
flea market are. It's with this thought that Billy finally stops in row three and
chats with one of the oldest market salesmen. "Good morning, sir. My name
is Billy." The old man reaches over and turns the dial on the radio to silence
the music of his generation. "Why, yes, yes, it is a good morning, young
man." Billy is encouraged by the man's welcoming tone. Billy asks, "Every
week, we see you here at the market, and I've been meaning to say hello, but

Keys to Success. *Artist, Shane Tomalinas.*

New Egypt Flea Market, established 1959. *Author's collection.*

Grandpa knows the lady on the other side, so we tend to walk that way. And you don't have much on the table for sale for us to look at your display. How come?" The burly old man moves to the side so Billy can get a better look at what's behind him.

There, sitting on a side table, is an old teal Smith Corona typewriter. "What's that metal thing?" Billy politely asks. "It's what I sell the most of," replied the smiling old man. Billy, looking dumbfounded, says, "You only got one of them and it's been here every time I come to the flea market. So, you haven't sold a thing then." The older man responds: "Ah, but you're wrong, young man, for I sell adventure. My business takes me around the world. And my customers are guided on great escapes through jungles, both concrete city jungles and the jungles of Central America. I'm a writer." Billy knows a thing or two about writers. He reads every chance he gets. Sounding older than his seven years, Billy exclaims with a quizzical look on his face, "They use computers to write the books I read. How come you use that old blue thing?" Now, it's the old man's turn to look quizzically at the young man. "My stories involve people. And people of all sorts come to the market, just like you. Here is where I get the chance to meet them, and my encounters turn into sentences of adventure on that antique typewriter for my next story. You see, meeting you today is like research. I might add you to my next big story. If I needed a fancy computer to tell a story, why, I wouldn't be able to fill my stories with wonderful characters that are sparked from real life."

"Welp, I gotta go. Nice talking to you, sir." Billy runs to catch up with his grandmother and grandfather. The old man turns to the vintage keyboard and begins to quickly press the letters "Billy." He looks up in the direction of the little boy he just met and hears, "Grandpa, that nice man is king of the adventurers. He's a writer!"

5

JERSEY DEVIL'S TRIANGLE IN THE PINES

Every good fairytale or urban legend is equal parts fantasy and fact. But they say truth is stranger than fiction. The following is a story that has been told for generations. It's about a real place that has an unreal occurrence. Like most fairytales, this story is caught between the past and the present. The truth is out there, but with each day, the suspect's trail grows cold. This local lore took root in the 1980s, possibly going back even further to colonial times. It goes between two old place names on a map: Davisville and Midwood. Place names are full of fantasy, as one generation replaces the names from the past. Davisville suffered from this line of thinking, as it has been known by several different names since the early 1900s. On more modern topo maps, it's listed as Archers Corner. Yet no one remembers the Davises or the Archers. Davisville exists today as only a weird county intersection with stoplights and stop signs in all directions. But the mysterious occurrence that is part of this tale takes place a mile or so south into the woods of Colliers Mills, where neither man nor beast dares tread. It is the Bermuda Triangle of the Pines.

In a world full of change, the only constants are the wind and the rain. A man builds a house and it stands with his family over the generations, but ultimately, it succumbs to time and is erased by weather or fire. A family name like the Archers' is left only in history books and on map labels like Archertown Road, Archers Corner and even an early four-walled schoolhouse named after them. A generation grows and withers like the corn planted in rows on a farm. No one remembers why that corner is named

The Jersey Devil. *Artist, Shane Tomalinas.*

Archers Corner. The new families who replaced the old scratch their heads at the names in the area and wonder why some names stick while others are changed over time. Some families migrate to new areas for work, while others leave to escape their past. If ever there was a place to hide in plain sight it would be between the dividing line of two small towns. Jackson Township and Plumsted Township, both of Ocean County, are divided by Hawkins Road, which intersects Archers Corner and is only a few miles as the crow flies from a strange place of legend called Jack Davis.

"Dad, I went hiking over the weekend at Colliers Mills Wildlife Management Area on a new hiking trail some folks put together called the New Jersey State Long Trail. It cuts through and parallels County Road 528—West Veterans Highway, I mean. You know the area? 'Cause I heard the strangest thing while I was out there hiking by myself." The mother enters the kitchen. "You don't want to be going out there. Don't go out there again! Jack Davis isn't safe. You heard the stories from your uncles the same one Dad told me." The raised eyebrows and looks of fear on the mother's face caused some concern. "What story did Pop-Pop tell you of the place?" This was one of those moments in life when one is being scolded for something by their parents, but they don't know why they're in trouble. "My dad told us kids to stay out of the area folks called Jack Davis, the area you're saying you hiked through. He came home with the hound dogs and his shotgun one day to the farm where we lived on Hawkins Road directly across from Colliers Mills. Usually, he'd walk up the street to Uncle Paul's and walk through his backyard and hunt the old cranberry bogs out there. This time, when he came back though, the worried look on his face had me scared. He sat all of us down—all five of us kids. Being a teenager, I had never seen that look on my dad's face before. He was afraid of something, and he was in the Navy—nothing scared him. He said to us he was out hunting like usual and got to a part in the swamp where the water was knee-deep in places coming from the Shannoc Brook, forcing him and the dogs to take the higher ground as they walked in between the swampy waters but also leading deeper into the swamp. You could hardly see around each turn. Well, they came to a point out there in Jack Davis where the dogs stopped walking. Dad couldn't pull them forward. Dad says, 'Lucky had his tail between his legs and was whimpering something fierce.' He felt a chill run down his neck like something was watching him from up ahead, but you couldn't see anything cause of the overgrown blueberry brush and swamp maples. Then, all of a sudden, he heard a screech or a scream—maybe it was a howl—but it scared the shit out of him, and he turned tail and ran out

An aerial photograph, circa the early 1980s, of the home of Frank Paul Emery and his wife, Carolyne Amanda Emery, at 165 Hawkin Road, New Egypt. *Author's collection.*

of there. The dogs didn't need no instructions, as they were in full escape mode and Dad could barely keep up with them."

Then the father joins the conversation. "She's not lying. Her brother Tommy said he saw something out that way when he and his brothers were hunting too close to where their dad had told them to stay out. He believed he saw a sasquatch or bigfoot. I never believed them, but your mom's dad hunted and knew Colliers Mills better than anyone, for he lived across the street all his life on the farm there. Jack Davis is a no-no. No one would even show me where the exact place was. And most wouldn't hike out that way, as it was hard walking being uneven terrain and you couldn't see anything as you walked through the swampy areas. One time, me and your uncle Richard were hunting, and we went out past Paul's house like your mom's dad did. We were out about a mile and the bogs opened in front of us. On the right side of us a mile or so was Stump Tavern Road and to our left a mile was the big bogs seen off Route 528. But out ahead of us were old, overgrown and abandoned cranberry bogs. Somewhere out there was where Jack Davis was. I guess the area was named for one of the squatters that lived along the old bogs—not sure. Used to be roads that you could drive out on, but now, the state's got the area cordoned off. So, we were standing there on one of those old roads with the sun just rising and off to the side of the road a ten-point buck, big [swear word] buck, was right in front of us. Richard wouldn't let me shoot as it was almost seven o'clock. You could walk through the woods, but you couldn't shoot until seven. As it neared the legal time to start hunting, the deer turned and went deeper into the swamp of Jack Davis. At seven, the deer was out of range from our guns and Richard wouldn't walk out into the bogs to try and get a closer shot at it. I mean, we had guns. What was going to hurt us? We lost the nicest buck you could want to Jack Davis."

Was there a sasquatch out there in Jack Davis? If it wasn't a bigfoot, what was it? Who was the area named for? Poking around in a few local history books produces a homeowner by the name of Ivins "Jack" Davis who lived in town. He was born in New Egypt in 1855 and died on July 19, 1928. He was the first president of the local bank. It's odd that a banker would own a land parcel that would ultimately become part of the state's wildlife management area. There's no proof that this notorious area of legend was owned by a banker. But there's also no proof of the existence of a squatter turned sasquatch named Jack Davis that could cause the bravest of men and hounds to turn tail and run. The area of Jack Davis is one that could sustain a creature of legend and its need to stay secluded. Locals believe the creature is real, but most don't even know where Jack Davis begins and where it ends. And yet, the sources of creatures of fancy could be narrowed down to a short, practical list. By the 1980s, a large beast that could put a fright to one, if encountered in a swamp, could possibly have come from two local sources.

Many residents of the Plumsted Township area would agree that, within its borders and the edge of Jackson Township, a Bermuda Triangle or Devil's Triangle exists. Colliers Mills has more legends than the popular mouse with big black ears. Ephraim Empson, who built a three-story hotel and a town within Colliers Mills, was the cranberry king of old. Coaling or charcoaling and the colliers who worked to make charcoal from burned timber littered the area in question. There was once a town called Success that Pine Barren authors wrote about. An untold legend took place on Hessian Island, a hideout of infamous Pine Robbers. Within the area of Davisville, Midwood and Colliers Mills—the Pine Barrens of New Jersey—that triangle stretches across nearly thirteen thousand acres of wilderness. And as the crow flies, there are two sources of unimaginable beasts. Usually, the public is the last to know when an exotic creature escapes. In 1974, the area was introduced to the Six Flags Great Adventure theme park and its popular Wild Safari, which literally backs up to Colliers Mills WMA. And another local source was only eight miles away as the crow flies: Tigers Only Preservation Society, in existence from 1969 to 1999, rivaled the Tiger King. In the end, the state shut it down. (Think very big, hungry cats!) The park made national news when, in 1999, a Bengal tiger escaped. Who knows what could wind up in a human-less void of the Jack Davis swamps of Ocean County? Of note, just twenty miles away in Howell, New Jersey, a Great Adventure baboon escaped and was captured in 2011.

Oh, and by the way, "What was the strange noise the author heard that was mentioned at the beginning of our story?" The Bermuda, or Jersey Devil's, Triangle in the Pines that exists today at the fringes of Plumsted Township and within Jackson Township is an enigma. No one of sound mind and body would dare to venture out into the knee-deep swamps of the once cranberry-filled bogs, where legends still live, breathe and stalk mankind. Logical explanations sound so illogical when they aren't based on facts, for the truth of the matter can't be explained away or proven within the Jersey Devil's Triangle of the Pines. And locals still tell tall tales. Maybe the ghost of ole Empson haunts the entire area, for his tragic death beneath the hooves of one of his prized racehorses would certainly cause a spirit unrest. Or maybe the rambunctious ghosts of escaped Hessian soldiers and callous Pine Robbers' souls search the swamps for places where forgotten treasures are still buried. But I can promise that if you spend a good amount of time hiking the blue-blazed trail of the New Jersey State Long Trail in the vicinity of Jack Davis, you might be able to re-create what the author heard. Another fanciful beast was the cause of the strange noise the author encountered at the beginning of our story. These wonderful beasts are villains of many fairytales, yet here at the edge of Devil's Triangle, they find a loving home. And one can visit their home and take a tour. But if you like to explore and find yourself on the blue-blazed trail near Jack Davis, listen for their howls. These weren't the sounds my grandfather heard that fateful day back in the early 1980s, as their howls didn't start until 2005. But when they are heard late in the evening, when your feet are standing on a pine needle–laden trail and, overhead, the dark boughs of pitch pine absorb the sun's last light, the howls of several wolves from Howling Woods Farm can send chills down your spine.[4] They will hasten a return to your parked car, an escape from who knows what is lurking in the shadows of Jack Davis and the Devil's Triangle of the Pines.

6

TOM THE TURKEY AND THERESA THE TURTLE

The white man has a name for the fire Mother Earth exhales before a blanket of cold covers the land. It's called Indian summer. On such a day, two old spirits collided on a mountain in southern New Jersey. They had been wandering the land separately, both being homeless. Fate found that their paths crossed on a mountain that some would call a molehill in the Forked River area. The white man's names for locations have no place in the hearts of these weary travelers who were destined to meet with the autumn winds at their backs and the rosy sun kissing their foreheads, bringing hints of sweat as they climb to the top of the mountain.

If it was a race to the future, neither Tom nor Theresa would say, for both had lived full and long lives to only wander aimlessly, disconnected from places that once held different names. And who would race to a future that didn't include them? Tom the turkey got to the top of the mountain first and took a near 360-degree turn: "It's almost the same as I remember it." From the east side came an old, raspy voice that startled Tom. "Brother, you live! But you stare at me as if you've seen a ghost." It's true. Tom the turkey did believe he was seeing a ghost, for there, on top of the mountain, was Theresa the turtle, part of the clan who stayed behind while Tom the turkey and others were scattered across the land. "The years have not slowed you, my sister, and your heart still is full of cider, giving you the energy to climb this ole mountain like we did as children many moons ago. Let us make a fire and sit so our old bones can settle."

Left: Turkey and Turtle. *Artist, Shane Tomalinas.*

Below: Forked River Mountain vista, April 2021. *Author's collection.*

No one would believe you if you happened upon a scene such as this: a turtle and a turkey working together to arrange a rock circle. After gathering wood, they set it ablaze on top of a mountain in southern New Jersey. Both the turkey and the turtle appeared weathered from their travels and worn down from the passage of time. It was a fortuitous meeting, as each nearing their hundredth moon made their way hundreds of miles to this very spot. And as the sun set, the moon rose above their last meeting place. Theresa the turtle's only notable feature was her face, which was colored a red that matched the flames of the fire they had just built. And if you had to describe Tom the turkey, well, he was tall and very lean for a turkey. They both sat cross-legged beside the fire and looked across the flames at each other. Each took turns talking about where Father Time went so hurriedly, how many of the clans' dreams were lost and how only a few remained to dream of a better future.

"Even in the dark, the white man's presence can be seen and felt from this height." droned Tom the turkey, pointing to a military hanger to the north.

"You ran like many of the clans to escape our homeland, only to find out that the fire of the white man could not be put out. I, too, have wandered far and wide but always stayed along the coast, never finding peace where once the land beneath us was not owned but given by the great creator," cried Theresa the turtle.

"It is here where you and I will find peace, for the searching is over. The days and nights are no longer numbered by the passing of the moons but the glow of the embers in this fire. But I do see the wisdom in your words, Theresa, my sister. It wasn't long before we who left for a better—no—quieter horizon realized your words of truth. It was too late to turn back. The white man is like black bear grease when it gets on your hands. No matter how many times you wash your hands, the grease remains. It takes many washings to rid yourself of the slippery feeling between two fingers." grumbled Tom the turkey.

"Yes, and we never found a way to wash them away, did we brother?" joked Theresa the turtle. Tom stared out at the horizon that had once been unobstructed by the flashing lights of a plane or a manmade tower and replied, "No, the wisdom we looked to the creator for never came."

The winds of change blew across the evergreen sea. If Tom or Theresa were an eagle, they would have enjoyed the thermals rising from the mountainside and been able to feel the winds on their face as they glided across the pine trees toward the ocean. Yet they were only a turkey and a turtle—landbound with no land to call home. It's a different kind of

The view at the top of Forked River Mountain, overlooking Ocean County, April 2021. *Author's collection.*

The view of Hangar I at Lakehurst from Forked River Mountain, April 2021. *Author's collection.*

An illegal campfire on top of Forked River Mountain, October 2022. *Author's collection.*

homelessness than what the white man's city folk experience. They were searching for a home that no longer existed. The grease wasn't just stuck under their fingertips: it covered their hands and leaked down their arms, past their elbows and onto their chests, seeping into their hearts. The pain of being a turtle and a turkey were nearly burned out. As a hefty gust of wind finally blew the last red coal from the fire out, the spirits of Tom the turkey and Theresa the turtle were extinguished there on Forked River Mountain, finally taking to the skies like eagles.[5] Their search ended on top of Forked River Mountain, but other turtles and turkeys are still out there, searching. We can only hope they find peace, too.

7

DANNY BOY NO MORE

It was a beautiful Indian summer afternoon in November when little
Dan went on a ride with his grandpa to the end of Seven Bridges Road.
The road's name is officially Great Bay Boulevard, but if you have any salt
in your hat, you know it's Seven Bridges Road.[6] However, every time you
drive the road and try to count the number of bridges, you always come up
one short for a total of six. Like all of man's crazy dreams, some are fully
realized, while others of shooting to the moon fall short and land in the
night sky among the stars. An afternoon of daydreaming got little Dan at
the end of Seven Bridges Road in a similar predicament. Yet he wasn't the
one who asked for it; his grandpa Joe had a way about him that some would
call unconventional. He'd slap you upside the head to teach you something
and make sure it would stick. In one story, Grandpa Joe's son Little Joe found
himself in a predicament after he grabbed a hound dog's bowl in the house
and wound up needing stitches. Grandpa Joe, ever the teacher, said to his
bleeding son, "Well, you won't do that again, will you?" Everyone—but a
child—knows that you don't get in between a dog, especially a hunting dog,
and its food, right?

The invite from Grandpa was innocent enough, as he stopped by
and asked little Dan, "Hey, Danny boy, you want to take the old 1975
International truck out to Seven Bridges and check out the bay, maybe dip
our toes in the salty water at the end of the road?" Dan happily agreed
after getting permission from Mom and Dad. What else did a twelve-year-
old boy have to do that would be as fun as hanging out with Grandpa on

Stick Shifting. *Artist, Shane Tomalinas.*

Rutgers University Marine Field Station. *Author's collection.*

a school night? The adventure started out with the sun on their backs, but by the time they got to the end of Seven Bridges Road, the sun was nearly down. The drive was about five miles out and five miles back. They got to see a beautiful sunset, and as Grandpa had promised, they got to dip their toes in the bay after a quick walk through the thickets to the beach at the end of Great Bay Boulevard. Wrapping up the adventure, they got to the truck just as the last light was leaving the East Coast behind. Grandpa Joe let the tailgate down, and they both jumped up and sat to take their shoes off and dump the beach sand out.

Once they were done, they hopped down, and Grandpa slammed the tailgate shut. Then off they went. The road was empty, as it is mostly an out-of-the-way place for adventure seekers or teenagers looking to have a beer and a smoke along one of the bridges of Seven Bridges Road. At each of the one-way bridges, there is a stoplight system in place. One vehicle on one side of the bridge waits at a red light while the oncoming traffic with the green light has the go-ahead to cross. It's very efficient, and with little traffic to begin with, it's a safe way to cross the one-way bridge system out to the bay. As Grandpa drove to the first bridge's red light, he turned down the country music station on the old AM/FM radio and put the International in park. Looking over and handing the keys to Dan, he said, "Well, I think it's about

Left: The trail at the end of Great Bay Boulevard, Tuckerton, New Jersey. *Author's collection.*

Below: One of the six bridges on Seven Bridges Road. *Author's collection.*

time you got a chance to take this old green bucket of rust for a spin. Don't you?" There goes Grandpa Joe again. "Grandpa, I'm only twelve. And I don't think I can see over the steering wheel, and this truck has a shifter on the floor. What do I do with that?" Dan looked like a cat dropped in a tub of water. Grandpa Joe said, "Hardest part of any job is getting started. That's what my dad used to tell me when we owned the farm. And I learned to drive when I was eleven on a bigger truck than this '75 Harvester with its V8. You'll be fine. Grab the keys and switch places with me. You drive the next few miles, minding to stop at the red lights for the next few bridges until we get the green light, and before you know it, we'll leave the salt meadows behind us and I'll take us home."

And off they went. Little Dan drove as Grandpa Joe strung lyrical sentences together in conversation, talking of his own days of youthful learning and how it compared to those of the youth today. All the while, he offered words of encouragement to Dan as the miles melted away before them. Grandpa thought it was a fine time for a teachable moment. But this twelve-year-old boy who had never driven before, especially a manual transmission in the dark, had to cross over bridges that, with one wrong turn, could plunge him and Grandpa to their certain deaths. Well, it was like the proverbial "toss the cat into the tub and see if it sinks or swims" moment. After the first green light and a nervous little boy's pounding heart that was seemingly louder than the country music on the AM/FM radio, little Danny boy took to driving that ole green beast like a duck to water. (No, not like a cat to water—but a duck.) Grandpa looked over his shoulder after the first bridge was successfully crossed with little Danny boy driving and said, "I reckon we left little Danny boy back there at the end of Seven Bridges Road. You're just Danny now." Beaming with pride, Danny drove on as Grandpa popped the top off an Old Milwaukee.

8

DEAD MAN'S CURVE ON JUNCTION ROAD

Many a Piney who's lived in the Pines has been subdued by what they call locally "Apple Jack." Pineys can trace the course of their history through the different races of men and women to see many tragedies caused by alcohol abuse. It's not a sole characteristic of Pineys or an ailment known only to them, but like many of our favorite campfire stories told late at night around a fire, alcohol is usually involved. In the Pines of old, they had a term for when men and women imbibed too heavily in Apple Jack: Apple Palsy. This state of being often comes when you try to buck the system with the belief that you can spit in its face and take the world on all by yourself. Drinking Apple Jack is an old Piney pastime. That drink has now been replaced by a greater array of evil spirits afforded by the common man that cause the same paralysis of the brain. Society's progress and its rules and laws are for others to follow—the rebels of the south (southern New Jersey) made their own rules. The following is a story of a man who suffered the same fate, yet in the end, it wasn't a bottle that killed him but Dead Man's Curve.

In the months of fall—September, October and November—Mother Earth is unrivaled in beauty when she's clothed in her modest and most elegant satin green dress with luxurious, silky red stockings. Take a spin on the highway at fifty miles per hour and you'll feel as if you're dancing the Latin salsa with this sexy lady. The roads of the Pine Barrens of New Jersey usually run straight from point A to point B, but there are some lovely spots at this time of year that offer a glimpse of Mother Earth's

Deadman's Curve. *Artist, Shane Tomalinas.*

Left and opposite: Black huckleberry in fall colors. *Author's collection.*

sexy curves. Just hop on Route 563, where the road touches the Mullica River along Lovers' Lane and then head north straight through the heart of the Pinelands and Chatsworth New Jersey. Along your drive, you'll see how flippant Mother Earth is with her satin green dress, bearing her legs covered in crimson red at every turn in the road. As you're speeding along the straightaway, you'll see her dress reaches the ground, carpeting the area with a brilliant red from the leaves of black huckleberry (*Gaylussacia baccata*). But as soon as you hit a turn in the road, where the highway skirts a bog or a swamp, she turns and spins in the most provocative way that only a salsa dancer can display. Her dress rises high up her eloquent body to display a swamp maple on fire, dwarfing the everyday green with bright red to match the color of the season. Once you round the bend, her dress hits the floor again, but each of those exciting turns in the road reveals her sultriness. All of this lures many men and women to the Pines to fall in love—with or without a shot of Apple Jack.

Such was the case of poor ole Joe Boy Britton. The laughable irony of life if it didn't involve death. He traced the same curves of the Pine Barrens for the last time. One day, racing time and a storied past, Joe Boy took to the roads of the Pines of southern New Jersey, as he often did. It seemed all his short life, he was chasing something but could never catch it. And like all rebels, he loved to end a race while polishing off a bottle of evil spirits. The race began like many others taken on by rebels without a cause—a fight or a snub of the law and off to prison. In Joe Boy's life, his greatest accomplishments left him in a prison suit. He spent his days stealing vans, firearms and motorcycles. His nephew remembers one night when Joe Boy showed up at the house with a new car and visited for a spell. The next day, while riding to work with a kindly neighbor, they stopped at Marshall's Corner in New Egypt, New Jersey. The neighbor wanted to show Joe Boy's nephew the car of the guy who broke into his house and stole his guns that the cops recovered. They found that Uncle Joe Boy was the one who stole a car and some guns, too. The family knew that while riding with Joe Boy, one could easily find themselves on the wrong side of the law. Joe Boy was living in the fast lane, speeding along the highways of the Pine Barrens and running, not from a woman in fiery red silk stockings, but from the red lights of the law.

Joe Boy's life was wasted on the highway, bucking the law and searching for the next love. He was always comparing the women in his life to the one with the evergreen dress and fiery red stockings from his childhood. Even poor Joe Boy, chasing his fate at ninety miles an hour with no braking in sight, began his wayward life at age seventeen, when he stole a car and stayed for free at the county jail. Not long after he got out of jail from his first visit, he went again for his second. He was a repeat customer, if you will. This time, he was jailed for brawling with two cops in Lakewood. With more time than most on his hands in a four-walled cell, Joe Boy prayed to start a new life with a new wife—who happened to be a preacher's daughter.

Above: Fall's fiery colors of black huckleberry, or *Gaylussacia baccata*. *Author's collection.*

Left: Swamp maple, or *Acer rubrum*. *Author's collection.*

Opposite: A field of autumn colors in the Pines. *Author's collection.*

After falling in love with the preacher's daughter and getting out of jail once again, Joe Boy moved to Browns Mills for a fresh start. Since the couple never had any kids and Joe Boy never kept a love interest for too long, the relationship was destined to end abruptly. The story is the relationship went to hell when our rebel robbed a casino in Atlantic City, adding to his time spent in the prison system. He was living the life of James Dean with less glamour and less sobriety.

It wasn't an ill-fated night like those at the beginnings of all great campfire stories that conclude mysteriously to help continue legends of old. And no, our hero wasn't brandishing a sword to save the girl from the Jersey Devil of lore, for she, with her satin green dress and fiery red stockings, needed no saving from the devil or the fires that burned in Joe Boy's eyes. He was a Piney man chasing his own demons. But this time, the evil spirits weren't at the bottom of a bottle—or a can, for that matter—as this story ends with the last dance of our antihero on the highway. Ironically, no spirits of the liquid variety were involved, but some unnatural occurrence did take place on that fated corner in southern New Jersey in 2001.

In the end, it wasn't a drunken Piney who went down in flames but a sober one, who went on an early morning motorcycle ride—not late at night like most legends of lore. It was a foggy autumn morning when his last dance began at the water's edge on Lovers' Lane, leaving behind the Mullica River for the last time and speeding down the highway ending in Browns Mills.

In another bit of irony, as if the Pines aren't full of bog iron to begin with, this was the very same road traveled when poor Joe Boy was laid to rest. In 2001, they laid his body in the Green Bank Cemetery at the same time terrorists attacked the World Trade Center in New York City. But we get ahead of our hero's story in our antihero's storied past.

Our rebel, back in the leather saddle, rode that motorcycle like there was no tomorrow. He danced as well as the legend of old Joe Mulliner, the Robin Hood of the Pines. Joe was a thief who met his end not on a road or a rail but a rope. Joe Boy's motorcycle danced for the last time with that sexy lady who wore the evergreen dress and thigh-high red crimson silk stockings in the chilly airs of

A discarded beer can. *Author's collection.*

the morning. No one ever escapes her beauty once it's been seen for the first time. On this day's last dance, Joe Boy, being no Robin Hood but a thief who couldn't steal any more time from Father Time, sped down Mount Misery Road to the corner of Junction Road in Browns Mills, nearing Dead Man's Curve. An unheard-of dense fog bellowed from the woods at Dead Man's Curve. If you were to walk straight into the woods at that fateful spot, you would eventually find yourself at one of the oldest iron forges of the Pine Barrens. Mary Ann Forge blew smoke from the hot coal-fed furnace, refining pig iron from Hanover Furnace along the Mount Misery Road. Locals say the uncanny mist that blanketed the area that fearful morning came from Mary Ann Forge's red, amber waters.[7]

Red is the color of the ill-fated life of Joe Boy Britton: red dress, red cedar waters, a red bottle of booze, flashing red lights and police sirens. His destination was his big sister's home on Junction Road there along the old Kinkora Branch of the Pennsylvania Railroad, only yards past that deadly corner. That morning, the visibility died down miserably. Joe Boy, with the need for speed, had his motorcycle dancing on the blacktop pushing ninety miles per hour, some say. They say there was no screeching sound from Joe Boy braking or rubber hitting the road, but there was a large bang that was heard up and down the quiet street. Our man in the black leather jacket took a bow, adding another soul to the reaper's count along Dead Man's Curve.

To this very day, some say when the autumn winds blow after the passing of the full moon, Dead Man's Curve becomes blanketed in heavy mist. Quietly standing on the corner in the chilling air, one can hear the large bang of a pot. Some say they have heard the ringing of the hammer in the woods out at old Mary Ann Forge. Many a Piney spent their lives at the forge till their dying days. Still others say they can hear the sound of the numerous crashes along that fateful curve echoing in the foggy morning and late night. They claim they are the spirits of those who could not outrun Dead Man's Curve. Who's brave enough to stand on that corner in the dead of night with fall's chill air clawing at your neck to see if it's the ghosts of the dead making the banging sound or if it's truly the giant hammer of Mary Ann Forge from the days of iron in the Pines?

9
LESSONS OF A SWEET CITY GIRL

The city vagabond shouted on the corner of a busy street in Philadelphia, "Do not look at me, for I am ugly, and I am not feeling my best!" An old woman nearing the same side of the busy street, using a cane to enter the crosswalk, replied, "It is not my job to make you feel better, nor is it my worry that you feel you are ugly." And with that, the man, who was standing on an old milk crate, got down from his high perch and went about doing what vagabonds do. As for the little old lady, she did not care one way or the other. She mumbled under her breath as she safely exited the crosswalk, "The kids these days want us to prop them up with pretty words because they weren't taught where true beauty exists."

Our sage made her way back to what she called her "backyard" with a cup of Earl Grey tea in a paper cup, which she planned to enjoy while sitting on a Philly park bench. I know what you're going to say: "What backyard?" In one of the East Coast's oldest cities, Mrs. Milly calls the public park near her tiny home her backyard. And she's had the same routine since retiring from the Philadelphia National Park Service twenty years ago. Washington Square Park is conveniently within walking distance of her little rented apartment. It's a tiny space she calls home but one that she can afford even after retiring from being a park ranger for nearly twenty-five years—all of which was spent in the City of Brotherly Love. Her preferred position on the bench is facing opposite the public walkway, staring out into the woods. An odd thing occurred this day to Mrs. Milly, as her normal routine was to sit quietly and enjoy her tea in peace, all the while staring into the nature scene

Mountain Laurel, *Kalmia latifolia. Artist, Shane Tomalinas.*

that changed like the channels on the TV, depending on the month of the year. She cared little for TV, but she loved with all her heart the serenity that nature provided, even in a city like Philadelphia.

"Hey, lady!" There was a tapping on Mrs. Milly's shoulder, so she turned and looked up at the man who was interrupting her serenity. There stood the preaching vagabond from earlier. "Are you stalking me?" She grabbed her solid cane. "Do I need to rap you over the head a couple times to shoo you away like a fly on a breakfast biscuit?" Milly didn't take any crap. City living creates a certain type of callousness in the goings-on around you, a kind of barrier of protection so that even in a street of one thousand people, you can still find a tiny space to enjoy peace and quiet. It just so happens that the vagabond was trying to ruin this lovely fall day. "No, no. I just wanted to ask you a follow-up question to our conversation from before." Mrs. Milly was ready for anything. "Well, it wasn't much of a conversation, but if you're going to stand there jabbering, ruining the quiet, at least sit down. What's your question? My tea is getting cold." Sitting as instructed, the man asked, "Well, I had one question, but now I have two after fortuitously finding you again. You're the only person who has ever said anything to me. All this week, I've been getting up on that box and preaching, and it was like no one even saw me—until today. Now, I find you in this lovely park, and you aren't people watching, as most people do in the city. They look at you, but they don't see you. If you know what I mean?" Taking a swig of her Earl Grey tea, Mrs. Milly answered, "You aren't from around here, are you? In a city like Philadelphia, brotherly love comes from not bothering your neighbor. In all that you just said, I couldn't find the question."

The vagabond's appearance wasn't disheveled like is typical of the other unhoused people you see in the city, and he was clean-shaven. Mrs. Milly had questions of her own, but she normally wanted to mind her own business and let the rest of her neighbors do the same. Living in the city, one adapts to their surroundings. Keeping your nose out of other people's lives is essential, for if you get involved in every passing preacher or unhoused person's business, you'd run out of time to enjoy your own peace of mind. That callousness forms a barrier that each city dweller carries with them. "The name's Ted. And you're right; I'm mostly a drifter but came to get the ashes of my dearly departed mother who lived in Philly all her life. You might have walked by her a thousand times, as this park, I was told, was one of her favorites. My first question was why do you face the trees and not the walkway?" Mrs. Milly, not letting her warm tea get cold, took another sip and then responded, "I see people all day long; it's a city after all. But when

I come out here to my backyard, I watch this scene as it changes with the seasons. You see that bush there?" She points, "That is mountain laurel from the New Jersey Pine Barrens. I was here the day they planted it. My first job as a park ranger was at Batsto in Hammonton, New Jersey, deep in the Pines, which I love to this very day."

"Oh, very nice. That makes sense to me. I'll be moving along shortly, hoping to hitch a ride out of the city and head south, as the weather's changed and it's getting too cold to be sleeping on a park bench. I know you haven't seen me here, because the police come around and shoo you away at night in this place. Odd that some parks are fair game to the homeless, while others are off-limits. Oh, my original question was why did you address my concern about feeling ugly and being depressed by saying you didn't care when you could have just walked on by?"

There you go again, Mrs. Milly, sticking your nose in other people's business, and here we are talking to a vagabond about God knows what because of it. "Your statement made me sad for you. And someone needed to tell you the truth about the matter. It's like that green plant there whose leaves are turning yellow now. It looks all spent, not something others might find as being beautiful, because the plants are in a dormant stage. You and

A typical Pinelands scene. *Author's collection.*

65

I go through stages throughout our lives, too. Come spring, that green bush will be full of pinks and whites and have no equal in beauty. I suppose you, too, have been seen in that light before or maybe in the future to come. But it's not the viewer who needs to see the beauty; it's the person looking out that should see it. Beauty comes from within, not from what society labels you as. If you believe what the doorman at the hotel over there [she points to the Washington Square Hotel] thinks of you is true, well then, you're a damn fool, for he's only seen you in your dormant stage. The same goes for the folks at this park. If they think this bush is ugly, that's their problem, not the bush's, for inner beauty still exists, even if the cruel world casts ill-placed judgments from a first impression. Understood?"

Straightening his hat the vagabond goes on, "It seems I'm all out of questions. I need to be heading south with dear ole Mom [he holds up a backpack], back to the Georgia pines, where I'll spread her ashes among the woods she cared for—probably as much as you, ma'am, for this here lovely green bush called mountain laurel."

"You say you're from Georgia, Ted? To take Mom back to the pines of her earlier days? Sounds as if she was a smart lady—a transplant like me in this city whose heart was buried out in the pines, mine in southern New Jersey and hers in the South." Ms. Milly fumbles through her purse, "Now, before you even start to protest, I won't be hearing any of it. You just happened to catch me coming back from the deli over yonder, where I only went to collect my lottery winnings. Don't judge this poor old fool, for I do like to play the lottery each week. I wound up winning $500. I'm not much on charity, but here are two crisp one-hundred-dollar bills. You do what you like with them, but I'd like to think you'd buy a bus ticket to Georgia and maybe grab something to eat, too. But most importantly, take that city gal's ashes out of the city and to home under those pines she loved so much. One day, I hope my grandkids will do the same with my ashes, spreading them across the pines around Batsto Village. This is not a gift for you but a gift from one mom to another. You need to stop standing on crates and get your life straight."

10

DOLL AND THE RAINBOW BRIDGE

When I was a young boy, my great-uncle would tell me stories that had been handed down from one generation to the next. One of the most unbelievable involved a not-too-long-ago deceased relative. Usually, these stories' accuracy is difficult to prove. The events that took place and the people involved are dead and gone. But in this instance, my great-uncle personally knew the people in the story you're about to hear. If a story lives on, there must be a thread of truth to it—right? You can guarantee there is a mix of half-truths tied to the story by the time the teller gets done sewing. Such a story from the 1960s, in its entirety, is here for you to read and believe if you want, and if you think it's too far-fetched, then dismiss it. In our family, we believe the rainbow bridge exists, for we can see it today—maybe not in the way that characters in this story did, but you can reach out and touch it today after a short drive through the Pines of southern New Jersey. Now, go ahead and listen to my great-uncle tell the tale of the rainbow bridge at the end of the road in Manahawkin, New Jersey.

As with most stories from the Pine Barrens of New Jersey, which touch the Jersey Shore, where fresh water mixes with salt water, this one holds an air of mystery. Maybe this is because these places have sacred forces that come together to bring life and death to those who live among the reeds of the bay. The coming and going of the tide is a given, but whether the tidings are good or bad is not. One day at the end of a dirt road in Manahawkin, one wave and a bulkhead seemingly crashed into each other with great force. My niece Linda, whom the adults called "Doll" at the age of twelve,

Not All Graffiti Is What It Seems. *Artist, Shane Tomalinas.*

was wandering down the dirt road as she always did when visiting for the summer. She walked to the end of the road, where the Bridge to Nowhere existed. There was not much trouble to be had back then, especially out on that dirt road that ended with a bridge that had been toppled and abandoned years earlier. One day, to her surprise, Doll ran into another girl of a similar age who was on the bridge with spray paint cans in hand. She had nearly completed a painting with an assortment of colors matching those of a rainbow as Doll came running up, screaming, "Hey, what are you doing? Stop that!"

The girl was dressed in a shirt and shorts with only one peculiar item of dress to be noted: a pair of leather moccasins. She replied to Doll, "It appears as if you believe you can control my actions by expelling hot air out of your big mouth." Not looking for a fight, Doll began backing away as the other girl came marching down from the bridge. But remembering her father, Doll said, "My father works for the state and is one of the people who must go around and clean up all the graffiti in the area—like what you did to the bridge here." The girl in the moccasin shoes retorted, "Well, your dad isn't here, or I'd offer a few words of apology. But to you, I will only offer my name. Hello, my name is Sue." Perplexed but already taking a liking to the girl in moccasin shoes, Doll said, "Hello, my name is Doll." The girl in the moccasin shoes started to laugh. Doll responded, "If I could ask, why did you paint the broken bridge with rainbow colors?" The girl replied, "Wait, you're named after a children's toy?" Not taking too kindly to being laughed at, with a fiery, red tint on her face, Doll exclaimed, "Yes! It's because my grandmother called me it when I was young, so it stuck. We Pineys love nicknames, it seems. And you can never outgrow them once they stick."

The girl with moccasin shoes saw that her laughter angered her new friend. "I'm sorry I laughed. Grandparents without thought can make us feel like babies sometimes—and even worse. My grandmother once told me I was like a Canada goose, 'They lost their way just like you, Sue, for they let themselves get fat from the white man's food and started living in the town ponds begging for white bread scraps, no longer able or willing to fly the great distances along the trail in the sky of their ancestors.' Some days, that statement is all that I think about, and it shames me very much." In the corner of Sue's eyes, moisture began to puddle.

Trying to desperately change the subject so that she didn't have to witness her newfound friend, Sue, crying, Doll said, "I see from your shoes—I mean moccasins—that you must be a Native American right." Sue looks down and back up to meet Doll's eyes. "Well, in my culture, when we say 'rainbow bridge,' which is what you've made the bridge to nowhere look like with the spray paint cans, we are talking about a bridge our pets cross to land in heaven when they die. Later, when we die, we will meet them there; in the meantime, they are there, whole and healthy, playing in the hilly fields." Sue dropped the empty can of spray paint on the ground and responded, "I'm native to the land here, but I'm unsure if I'm Native American. And to correct you, they are not your pets; they are our companions here on Mother Earth. But I believe as you do that this bridge is the rainbow bridge. And it will take our companions to the other side, where we will be reunited with not just our domesticated animals but all the spirits of creatures, like the turtle, mouse, raccoon, deer and so on." Doll replied anxiously, "I didn't say this was the rainbow bridge, just that it reminded me of that." With calmness and look of one thousand years, Sue replied, "This is our rainbow bridge. You'll see. For I believe I've found the way."

"Have you ever been to the other side?" Doll's eyes got wide with curiosity. "You mean the other side of the creek, where the bridge picks back up again?" Sue said, "Yeah, I have a canoe. You want to go check it out?" The two girls, not yet teenagers, started running, and Sue grabbed Doll's hand—they were off on an adventure. Giggling and out of breath, now at the water's edge below the old remnants of the Bridge to Nowhere, Doll asked Sue, "The canoe is aluminum—don't Indians travel in wooden canoes?" Frowning now, Sue barked, "You're starting to sound like my grandmother." Doll said, "I didn't mean it that way, Sue!" Laughing again, Sue joked, "One day, my white man's canoe will turn into a dug-out tree trunk canoe of old, and I'll be on my way to the other side of rainbow bridge." Doll jumped in the boat as Sue pushed the canoe from the banks of the creek and jumped into the stern. The creek in this section, even at low tide, is easily passable in a canoe, and the distance between one bank and the next is but a few yards, not miles. So, with a short paddle, they made it safely to the other side.

As they approached the opposite shore, Sue tapped Doll on the shoulder and put a finger to her lips. They quietly landed on shore and hauled the canoe up the bank in stalk mode. Doll wasn't sure what they were stalking, but she mirrored the hunched-over posture of Sue and crept up the bank to view the bridge from the opposite end, which she had never seen before. Sue was nestled along the south side of the bridge to see the exact spot where she last stood while spray painting the bridge with rainbow colors. Doll got down next to her and looked in the direction Sue pointed. There, she expected to see the handiwork of Sue's spray paint replaced not by a gaping hole in the bridge but a full bridge that a car could drive over. As Doll opened her mouth, Sue clasped her hand around it and knelt, forcing Doll to do the same. They turned to view the bridge again, and Doll's eyes became wide with wonder at what she saw. Streaming across the rainbow bridge were animals of all sorts. But they weren't what Doll considered normal animals. She could see tiny sewn patches on them, and something else was off about them. They looked ghostly white and gray. Not one had color to it; the only color came from the vibrant spray-painted bridge beneath their paws.

Minutes turned into an hour as the girls sat and watched the animals come across the Bridge to Nowhere. As they came across the bridge, one by one—raccoons, squirrels, possums, deer, you name it—all had patches in different places on their bodies; as soon as they got to the last plank on this side of the bridge taking their first step on the marshland ahead, they vanished. Doll's mind raced as she sat next to her new friend Sue, watching a magical migration of what appeared to be ghosts—only the ghosts were animals. Just as Sue had described it to her before, it was a rainbow bridge that guides the dead companions of Mother Earth to heaven, not just cats and dogs. Doll had so many questions to ask Sue, but when she went to open her mouth Sue raised her finger again to her lips. Thus, they sat holding hands, watching for an hour there along the bay in southern New Jersey. Nobody else in the world would believe this, and there was no one around to prove it happened. But it was happening, and Doll's heart was overjoyed.

Hours seemed to pass as the girls watched the animals walk over the rainbow bridge. It was near sunset when Sue tugged on Doll's hand and motioned her to pull back; they remained hunched over as they crept down to the canoe. Without saying a word, they both righted the canoe and shoved off to the west bank. After stepping onto shore, Doll turned and saw that Sue had drifted a few feet back into the creek's channel, directly in the middle of both banks and the uprights of the Bridge to Nowhere. Above Sue was thin air. It was as if the bridge they had seen on the other side wasn't there. Doll cried, "Where are you going, Sue? What did we just see across the bank up there on the rainbow bridge? Those animals with the patches, why did they look like someone sewed the holes in their bodies up?" Paddling forward, closer to Doll but not close enough for her to be able to grab the bow of the canoe. Sue's face was glowing from the sun setting on Barnegat Bay. She took a moment and, after gathering her words, answered, "Doll, I do see why they call you that now. You fit the name, for you're as beautiful as the sun shining through the needles of those pinewoods that meet the bay. I knew I could trust you with my secret." Doll wondered and asked, "What secret? Come and get out of the creek before you get swept away by the outgoing tide."

"When we met today for the second time, it was fate. I had not known before my destiny would merge with yours, that fate would bring us together again. You see, the story I told you of my grandmother calling me a lost goose was true, but I left out the rest of the story—the rest of my story. That same day, I ran down this road to the Bridge to Nowhere and leaped from the top into the water below, intentionally drowning myself, for I had lost my way. Grandmother's words may have been mean, but they were true. I did not know who my ancestors were, and many of their traditions were lost to me. My spirit has wandered this road every day since. It was nearly a dozen years—maybe more—until one day, I saw you and your dad. You were just a babe, sitting in a car seat in his county work truck, and he was just starting a new job, full of pride, helping keep places like this free of graffiti. It was he who gave me the idea to paint the bridge in rainbow colors and find my way back. Fortuitously, just yesterday, a wayward gang of kids left their garbage behind, and it contained a whole box of discarded but full cans of spray paint. This bridge is my offering to right the wrongs of my ancestors and make amends for taking my own life." Doll stood frozen, fearing any move would make the mirage of Sue disappear just like the magical rainbow bridge. Whispering, Doll asked, "Find your way back to where?"

Sue's face was lit up like a sunflower in the rays of the setting sun. "Back to my people. The ones who walked this land before the white man—a girl named Sue whose only tie to her past culture was a pair of moccasin shoes. I was just as lost as so many animals whose spirits traveled the white man's highways after being hit by a car or a truck, stopping their life's light in an instant, death dealt while being blinded by the light of man's metal machines. My life was blinded by the white man's ways, leaving me lost, walking among

An author selfie at the Manahawkin Bridge to Nowhere. *Author's collection.*

people who were not my own. Taking my own life left my spirit wandering along man's road to the Bridge to Nowhere alongside many of the animals' spirits that also were left wondering the white man's roads. They wear patches where the one we call Earth Mother sewed them back together. The spray-painted rainbow now covering the bridge was created using the magic left behind by my own drowning in this very spot. My encounter watching your father erase the words of others on the Bridge to Nowhere gave me a way to right my own spirit. I found a new purpose and found myself with the discovery. That new purpose is to guide other lost souls taken too soon by the white man's ways using the power of my death and painting the bridge with blazing colors for others to crossover. You don't know how good it feels to be connected to your people and not be lost after forever wandering highways of pain and suffering brought on by the white man's design." While Sue turned the bow of the canoe, her words wrapped around Doll's chest like the girl was giving her a loving embrace. In an instant, the white man's aluminum canoe turned into a wooden canoe. Sue looked over her shoulder and blew a kiss to her friend Doll.

Startled by a truck horn, Doll used her arms to prop herself up and look across the creek, up to the Bridge to Nowhere. A man's voice was yelling her name. Shaking her head of the fog experienced when one first wakes from a restful sleep, Doll shouted, "I'm over here, Dad!"

"Girl, you know it's near dark. You'd never make it home in time for Mom's supper. And you'd wind up grounded, to boot, for being late." Looking around at the bridge and back to Doll, her father continued, "Well, look at that; some jerk painted the Bridge to Nowhere in rainbow colors. I'll have to come back tomorrow in the daytime and cover that up." Running up from the bank, Doll jumped into her father's arms. "Dad, please don't cover up the rainbow bridge." He responded, "It's my job to erase all the hate messages and graffiti folks paint on old relics like the bridge here in the county." Doll looked up at her father. "Those colors aren't filled with hate; they lead us to a better tomorrow." Her father shook his head and acquiesced. "No one will see it out here anyways, hidden in plain sight. Only drifters and teenagers run out this way from time to time—a road for the lost I guess." They got in the truck and started to pull away. Doll looked out her window as the last rays of the sun hit the bridge, and she countered, "Not all who walk the white man's roads are lost. And not all bridges are what they seem."

11

DEVILISH GOOD TIME FIDDLIN' DOWN AT BRINDLE LAKE

At the edge of the Brindle Lake, Joey thought he was going to make sweet music that night. "I know it's cold, Baby, but I didn't have enough time before tonight's gig to gas up. We're out in the middle of nowhere, and I don't want to run out of gas." He turns the car off. "Come closer, and I'll keep you warm!" It was a typical night for Joey, who played the fiddle and sang lead in the local bars. His melancholy music and honeycombed harmony almost always attracted a bar gal's eyes, and his personal charm took over from there. He grew up in the Pines and loved to sing the old ballads of Merce Ridgway and the Pinehawkers. Shortly after arriving at the lakeshore, where the two barroom lovers were rounding third base, a sound from the lake stopped them dead in their tracks, as if the runner just ran into the catcher at home plate. The two of them both looked at each other and simultaneously said, "Do you hear that music playing?" Not wanting to lose all the momentum he had strummed up thus far, Joey agreed to get out of the car to see what the fuss was. He said, "Probably another country boy out here singing his girl a song!"

He quickly got out of the car, and the heavy Cadillac door swung shut behind him before he could grab the flashlight from the dashboard. Looking around in the dark of night, he could see a light coming from across the way. He walked to the front of the car, which was parked and pointed in the direction of the lake. There, across the lake, near opposite him, stood a figure—or maybe two—but the damn moon had just dipped behind a cloud, and he could barely make out their outlines. The ripples on the lake echoed the soft

Left: Fiddlin'. *Artist, Shane Tomalinas.*

Below: A landscape photograph of Brindle Lake in Plumsted Township. *Author's collection.*

melody he heard before. What made Joey even more curious was that the exquisite melody had to be played on a fiddle, which is an instrument he knew better than most in these parts. With more curiosity than fright, he hurried back to the side of the car and opened the door to reach for the flashlight. To his surprise, he saw the car was empty. "Now, where the heck did that woman of mine go?" He thought to himself as he grabbed the flashlight.

Not missing a beat, he quietly shut the door, turned the flashlight on and started making his way east and then south on the fern-laden trail that traced the lake's edge. As he went, the minutes passed, giving him time to think back. He had picked up the woman, who's now gone to who knows where, after his last fiddle set of the night at the local bar. "What was her name again? Sally, Suzy, Sara maybe?" Joey was not much of a good man. Sure, he could play the fiddle and sing like no other, and it surprised most folks when they heard him play, for his alcohol-laced cologne and his wrinkled blue flannel shirt half tucked into his faded blue dungarees never gave the impression that he was good at anything. When Joey reached the clearing that was near opposite his Cadillac, the moon burst out from behind the only cloud in the sky, and there stood a woman holding a fiddle that looked as if it had been expertly carved from a seasoned ash tree trunk.

Dumbfounded, Joey blurted out, "Sara, how did you get over here? And how come you didn't tell me you could play the fiddle?" How she had snuck around to the other side of the lake and held a tree trunk of a fiddle that looked as if the strings were smoking while she played that sinful melody was a mystery to ole Joey. Most women he picked up at the bar after wowing them all night with his fiddle playing never got the drop on him like this gal had. He stood there with his mouth agape as he admired the fiddle that appeared to have initials scraped into the wood grain, right under the bridge that held those sinfully singing steel strings. The initials were "E.P." Come to think of it, Joey remembered a famous fiddler who was said to have played out here at Brindle Town with those initials. That famous Piney fiddler was none other than Ellis Parker.[8] Some believed it wasn't the fiddler of Piney lore Sammy "Buck" Giberson who won a fiddle-off against the Jersey Devil but the local hero Ellis Parker of Burlington County. Ellis played every weekend at the Brindle Town Pavilion one hundred years ago, and his initials were E.P. Now, here stands a strange woman at Brindle Lake with those same initials carved into a magnificent fiddle.

Dead calm settled over the lake as the woman stopped moving the bow of the fiddle, and the eerie quiet covered the shoreline where these two destined bodies stood. "The name's not Sally, Suzy or Sara, you fool. And you're one of the biggest fools I've lured out here for sure. You make it too easy. Men are so vain. I see you admiring my newly acquired fiddle—well, newly acquired to me, as I've had it for only the last eighty-six years. I'm just warming up to it. Most Pineys used red maple to make their fiddles but not this guy. He was just like you—so vain, so full of himself—which made it all too easy to steal his soul. And by the way, the name's Sadie. Some call me Sadie from Hadie, which I kind of like, as it has a nice ring to it, and it pays homage to my homeland of Hades. Others call me the Devil or the Jersey Devil in these here parts." Gritting his teeth now, his face full of concern, Joey asked, "Wait, wait, the Jersey Devil is a winged and hooved beast, not a witchy woman." Cackling laughter bounced across the lake. "You think I could keep setting the same trap for you gullible men to fall into if the truth got out that I, the Jersey Devil, was a handsome woman?"

The woman continued, "Here's an irresistible proposition I have for you, because I've seen no other as beautiful as you. And if you're as good of a fiddle player as you are a kisser, then I think you'll probably beat me in this game. And by the way, since we know each other's god-given names and are on a first-name basis, well, I feel I can correct you and not hurt your poor little man feelings, for your ignorance is showing. You're as ignorant as Ellis Parker and the hundreds of men before him. I'm not a witch, for the witches have but an hour to do their witching. My power comes in October—not just one hour of the day but an entire month. I have nothing against witches, for some of my best friends are witches. And I do love a witches ball!" With the sound of the word *ball* echoing across the brindle waters that give it the name Brindle Lake, Joey was lifted from the ground and enveloped in a giant ball of water centered in the middle of the lake. He was suspended just above the tiny island in the dead center of the lake alongside his date turned Jersey Devil. Both stood dry within the witches ball, and there was just enough room for two people to play a fiddle or two. "To host a witches ball and not invite guests would be so rude of me, don't you think?" Joey turned and looked around the lakeshore, now illuminated by the full moon, and saw hundreds of figures step out of the woods and onto the lake's shore. They were ghostly men, all carrying fiddles. Some wore their fiddles on their backs, and others dragged them on the ground like sacks—well, all but one. One face caught Joey's attention, because he had seen it in an old Piney book of lore. It appeared to be none other than Ellis Parker with a sad look on his face. If you know of Ellis's fall from fame, which landed him in the Lewisburg Federal Prison, where he died, you'd not be surprised to find him in the company of men who lost their souls to the devil.[9]

A portrait of Brindle Lake in Plumsted Township. *Author's collection.*

As the faces of bested men from the dawn of time came forward, the shoreline of Lake Brindle became overcrowded. It looked as if it were the Belmar or Asbury Park beaches in the summer instead of a lake in the woods in October. Sadie from Hadie pointed out, "I bet you thought the Devil was bested by the likes of Sammy Giberson or Ellis Parker. Those fool Pineys were left to live on to tell the tall tale that helped set the trap for my next victims. You get to play your songs, drink your wine and continue to lie to the girls about how you met the devil and he played the fiddle second best!" Joey, suspended over the middle of the lake with a devilish woman and surrounded by the ghosts of failed musicians, looked like he was about to be seasick.

Seeing the look on the face of her next victim, the Jersey Devil uttered, "Umm—I mean my next competitor. I let the likes of Sammy Giberson live and tell his lies after he signed the deed to his soul, like I promise to do for you when I beat you in a fiddle-off—a game of chance. You men seem to love to gamble, so why not? Don't fret, you've got nothing to worry about. It's not as bad as it sounds. Your life is riddled with rhymes and good times, balanced on a piece of worn wood with four singing strings. Even if you lose and I get your soul, you've still got a long life to live that any fiddler would die for. And like most men who gamble a lot, you know you win some and you lose some. If you win, you'll keep your soul, but if you lose, you'll live to tell the tall tale of how you met the Devil in the New Jersey Pine Barrens and bested him with your masterful fiddle playing." The lake's surface rippled below as the devil laughed aloud.

Out of thin air, Joey Horner's wooden fiddle appeared in his hands. Inspired, as the adrenaline and testosterone filled his body, Joey recalled an ancient tune that only Pineys of South Jersey would know. He played and played for nearly thirty minutes, and as his hands made quick work of the strings, the song filled the air. The ghosts on shore were cheering him on. In Joey's eyes, there was a glare or a shine that one could only describe as a fool gone mad. As the other men cheered him on, Joey forgot who his opponent was, and his strokes of the bow became brasher and more brazen. The piercing wail from the humming strings came to a crescendo that suddenly came crashing down as three of the four strings broke. "Ah, the 'Air Tune' ole Sammy Giberson tried on me back in the 1800s. Sammy, you out there?" A long-bearded man came forward, stepping into the lake water. "'Tis a good tune, I'll give you that. And no one has played it as well as you—except Sammy there. But it didn't work then, and it's not going to work tonight!"

Albert Music Hall, Waretown, New Jersey. *Author's collection.*

If there was another living soul at Brindle Town that night, they would say they heard an ungodly sound after poor Joey finished his turn at the fiddle and the devil began her twang. Naturally, it was ungodly for the people of the Pines, who refuted good Quaker living for the sins of the Pines and good times over yonder under Brindle Town Pavilion on Friday and Saturday nights. This left no room for any deities—other than Sadie from Hadie, also known as the Jersey Devil. The whiskey palsy experienced from having danced one too many jigs and having imbibed gallons of Apple Jack was the only way to forget the night you lost your soul to the Jersey Devil of old. She may be old, but the lure of her curves is undaunted, and the strings of her fiddle play like fire in the Pines—crackling hot. To this day, it's a bit uncanny how easy it is for her to find a fiddle player in the Pines willing to give up their soul for a one-night stand. If you asked any bluegrass band of the twenty-first century that played at Albert Music Hall in Waretown, New Jersey, what the most difficult thing about assembling a bluegrass band is, their response would probably be, "It's so darn hard to find a fiddle player!" Maybe that's why Sadie lets the defeated fiddle player continue to play until their dying day. She can wait to collect their souls, but good fiddling and good music can never die. Grandma might have been wrong when she cursed and said, "Rock-and-roll music is the devil's music!" From the mouths of past fiddle players like Sammy, Ellis and Joey, maybe it's really bluegrass.

12

SARA'S FROND UNFURLS

L ife's not so bad when you're too little to go to school and too little to get a job. But what's a kid to do while Mom and Dad both go to work each weekday? Why naturally, they go to Granny's house. She's what the poor call the next best thing to affordable childcare, as she's free most of the day and her time don't cost a dime. And if we're being totally honest, she probably needs childcare as much as the child; she's getting up there in age, nearing her ninetieth year on Earth. Still, having a purpose in life helps make life worth living, even if it's only to watch little Sara while Mom and Dad struggle to make ends meet. There's also a more fruitful purpose to child and elder time that isn't as apparent from the outside.

"Granny, you told Mom last night that you ain't just getting old 'cause you been getting old since the day you were born. What's that mean?" Here's the fruitful purpose we all are innately given on this Earth—the one that is given to each of us. Some take it up as a profession, while others refuse to share their knowledge and wisdom. Yet the best teaching comes from generational life lessons. You know, the things handed down from generation to generation—not just the knickknacks on an old bookshelf but the life lessons that are gathered over the years like a fine record collection. There are songs that stretch across a lifetime, and the sweet melody, when sung and shared with the next generation, creates a type of harmony that is one of the most fruitful purposes of life. Some songs are sad, while others are songs of hope. Granny is full of both, and she shares them daily with little Sara, who will pick up some of the songs and add them to her own collection alongside

Time Marches On. *Artist, Shane Tomalinas.*

her life experiences over the years. While the songs Granny sings are hard-earned tunes to her, they are easily gifted life lessons to little Sara.

Granny, sitting in her favorite and only wooden rocking chair, looking like an antique herself, looks at the child who reminds her so much of herself. Granny responds, "It's true, child, for the day you were born was the youngest you'd ever be. The arms of the clock march around in a circle, and with each passing moment, our bodies die a little. It's not the way you want to look at life, that's for sure. They'll teach you in school that you're growing. But really, we are all dying inside with each twirl of the clock's arms. But when you get toward the end, like me, where your life's band has been marching for so long toward the opposite end of the beginning, well, you get a different perspective on things." Sara never once complains to her parents when they say she's got to go to Granny's house and when they tell her to behave for Granny; she always says she will behave for a trip to Granny's house out in the Pines. These trips are just marvelous, and Granny is her favorite person in the world. Sara started to frown, looking a little down from what Granny had shared. "It's OK, little one, to count the days till your birthday as if the arms on the clock will go on forever, but we must recognize that each of us is dying. The fern in the yard grows each year from a tiny sprout like you and regrows to an old witch like me before it returns to the earth in the fall. You and I are like ferns. We're growing and dying at the same time. It's life and what's meant to be. You know what though?" Granny asks with a big grin.

Little Sara looks over, her frown replaced by a glowing smile she wears so well, and says, "No. What Granny?" Granny responds, "Granny learned the marching band may keep marching only if it eats! It may be getting to be fall, for the bracken ferns are turning yellow and brown, but you and I this past spring went fiddlehead hunting, didn't we?" Remembering as Granny said, Sara says, "We did, Granny, we did!"

"Well, I took out a small batch from the freezer last night for our supper." Sara said, "You mean lunch, right Granny?" Granny's face caught the glow of little Sara's and reflects the child's smile. "Supper, lunch, whatever you call it—it's gonna be delicious!" After they prepare the batch of fiddleheads together, each sit at the table behind a large, steaming bowl.[10] The bowls contain moist, green, earthy fern heads dripping with butter, garlic and salt. Sara looks over the kitchen table to Granny with steam rising around her cherub face and says, "The fern has so much to teach us, right Granny?" Granny, raising her nose from her bowl of steaming fiddleheads, savors the smell of Mother Earth and replies, "Its life gives us hope and nourishes our body, indeed. I may be the closest to the fall version of the yellow and brown

Left: Ostrich fern. *Author's collection.*

Right: A fern's frond unfurled. *Author's collection.*

bracken fern in the yard and you closest to the green fiddleheads we are about to enjoy. Alas, it is the circle of life." Slyly, Sara sits silently in her chair and shockingly lets a burp slip out. She covers her mouth with one hand and, giggling, blurts, "Granny, excuse me, but life is tasty!"

13

SIGNED WITH LOVE, PINEY GHOSTHUNTER

The changes of the seasons late in the year in America bring life to local legends that are retold time and again to invoke fright. Why is it that we as a species have the need to be scared and shaken by the unexpected popping up of a plastic skeleton in a gory, decorated neighborhood yard during Halloween? Nearly every town has a home where a local historian will take people on a ghost tour just to meet the demand for this type of enjoyment. If you stop and think about it, where do the ghosts hide all year long when it isn't ghost-watching season? Maybe we are fascinated by what we cannot see because each of our brains is designed to hide the ghosts that sit beside us.

She is not the spitfire woman I knew growing up. Back then, I would look to the *Webster Dictionary* to find a word to best describe her, but I came up short with only the word *opinionated*—for she was that and then some. Today, she is the ghost that lives among us like so many others that freely live among the living. I will not name her, for she is only one example among many. Ghosts are shells of the people they once were, living with diseases that physically removed, one at a time, pieces of the people they were. Unlike husking an ear of Jersey corn, where what remains is the best part of the plant, these life-altering diseases removed the essence of the human beings we loved, leaving us with ghosts—or husks—of our loved ones, just passing memories floating in the air. Look around and you'll find many living ghosts in your own life. Unless you live on a one-person island, there is truth to these words that you've yet to discover for yourself. We innately fear ghosts, because our mind shields our hearts from the loss of the living right before our own eyes. That premature loss brings a hurt we cannot emotionally carry, no matter how strong you may think you are.

From the outside, ghosts look to be the people you remember. And your mind, like an antique VCR player, pulls out a tape or two and hits the play button, giving you the illusion that a person who no longer exists is standing in front of you. These living ghosts frighten us beyond any horror movie creation, for if we could see the reality that exists in front of our faces and see these living ghosts for what they are, we would come to the realization

Tricks in the Dark. *Artist, Shane Tomalinas.*

that we are staring in a mirror. No one can stop time, and all around us, we can see how time is affecting the characters who play over and over in those home movies. They are characters reading from a script, and yet the lines in the script of today have changed so drastically that the original movie now feels foreign—that is if we are brave enough to stop and compare what once was and what life has become. These ghosts are eerily translucent, as if the living body is shimmering and trembling from the effort to stay within the boundaries of this world or be torn away entirely, shifting to the next plane of existence.

It's best we forget what we have read here and allow ourselves to be tricked by our own minds. There is no harm in attending a ghost tour of a haunted house during the pumpkin spice latte season. Nor does it hurt to celebrate all things spooky on all Hallows' Eve (more traditionally known as Halloween), when the children come around dressed as ghosts and ghouls, replacing the image of the ghosts you live with with fanciful costumes and cheery little makeup-covered faces. Thus, our minds and bodies play along with the façade, ever protecting us from the sadness that exists in the world. But once you see a real-life ghost, you will never see life the same again. You will become a believer that ghosts are real and do exist. Hollywood calls them spirits, but we know them for what they are: memories of loved ones who don't act or behave like themselves, for they've been taken away bit by bit, becoming living ghosts hiding in plain sight. Our hearts may ache, but we love them all the same. May their memories ever haunt our lives on this plane and the next.

14

GUARDIAN OF THE PINES

THE HERMIT OF OSWEGO

The reporter had a hot lead on the last living hermit in southern New Jersey. Their location was not to be disclosed for fear of another news agency getting the story first. As all best leads do, this one came in the wee hours of the morning at a local dive bar in the Pines, where a drunken Piney spilled the beans. The easiest way to spot a reporter in a bar is to look for the person buying others' drinks while only sipping on cold sarsaparilla. Many not-so-kind phrases describe these types of folks, like "fly on a wall," "flies swarming fresh roadkill" or "the ones found in the stall of a Port-a-John," but they are all found in the same dirty places. But the story is what matters most of all—how you get it is just part of the job. The drunken Piney had been hunting deep in the Pines where he heard his granddad tell him he shouldn't.

He told the reporter, "Hell with Granddad. He's dead and gone, and I wanted to tag a white stag of old legend. And I'd become a legend myself. It would be easy to spot as a few years back; the whole area was burned by a bonfire set by some fools." With bravado, the man revealed he had seen the beast he suspected roamed this hilly area out in Penn State Forest. After seeing it, he let not one but two shots loose; he thought he had downed the mystical beast. The fly interrupted the drunken Piney. "Wait, you did this last month? It was August and not hunting season." The drunken Piney retorted, "You a cop or something? If I don't listen to Granddad's words, you think I care about the law's words? I even took the shot balancing my gun on the door of my truck—damn good shot, too." After thirty minutes

Great White Stag. *Artist, Shane Tomalinas.*

of alcohol-laced banter, it appeared the man either missed or was mistaken, but his story revealed an even more intriguing and delicious tale: that of the last hermit of the Pines.

"I hopped out of my truck and ran across to the hill area where I saw the stag last. I had to run, as it was getting dark and I had only a 2-D flashlight handy. Once I got to the top of Spring Hill, I saw a fire that had been obscured from my vision back at my truck. The area had grown back quite a bit since the fires in 2019. There stood an old man wrapped in a fur coat, wearing a hat and carrying a stick—no, a staff—that looked as thick as Chatsworth's town flagpole!" The fly interrupted again. "Did you shoot the old man by mistake?" Plucking an ice cube out of the vacant Jack Daniels glass and tossing it nonchalantly in his mouth, the drunken Piney said, "I'm a damn good shot. There was no deer in sight, and the appearance of the old man damn near made me shit my drawers. If I hit him with one of those rounds, he didn't seem any worse for wear. He didn't say a word, come to think of it. Behind the pit fire, his glassy green eyes glowed. I was afraid I had shot him. But when he lowered that damn tree trunk of a staff and pointed it at the trail I came from, well, I lost all thought of a deer and ran back to my truck. I never told another soul about that hermit before except you."

As mystical as the great white stag was, the infamous appearance of a hermit that guarded the Pines area five miles northeast of Oswego Lake outside Chatsworth was just as enticing. This news was a gem the fly could use to gain respect from his coworkers at the paper. What the fly didn't know was that this adventure would lead him down a road littered with sticky fly paper. With a hot lead on a story, a good reporter never waits. The reporter was up early, and his plan to get to the area in daylight was much better than the drunken Piney's was, especially if there was a possibility of encountering a seven-foot-tall, silver maple tree–wielding legend. His directions were spot on, even though the GPS service was spotty along the drive, and the fly almost got lost as he crossed Bear Swamp Hill.[11] But just as he was pulling into the turnaround, there in the road ahead was a majestic white beast, as if it anticipated his arrival. Its shoulders had to be as tall as the cab of the truck. It appeared in a split second and was gone the next, leaving the reporter with no chance to even pick up his camera. After the reporter parked the truck and got out, there at the fly's feet were spent shotgun shells, right near the rutted road where the Piney must have parked late the previous month and illegally tried to kill that magnificent white beast from the front seat of his truck. "Who would want to shoot such a magical creature? Well, I would have loved to shoot it with my camera, but that's different." There were no other cars or trucks in sight, but you could see the incline to the hill, which, in the Pines, look like mountain tops. The sun had been rising as the reporter got on the road to leave Oswego Lake; now, it was fully up in the sky, its rays piercing the forested trail and hilltop where the reporter's destiny waited.

Even though the area had caught fire after some illegal activity in 2019; years later, it had a feeling that it was untouched by man. Wondering to himself, the reporter thought the drunken Piney's granddad and others must have held this area in awe and bestowed it a certain level of reverence, which is often ignored by the youth of today. Maybe it was out-of-towners who set the bonfire, or maybe it was the drunken Piney who gave the fly a bit of honey with the lead to this story, but either way, this was the place. Still wondering about the sight of the white stag and where it could have run to hide and be kept safe during the wildfire that blazed the area, the fly prepared to depart. The fly advanced with his camera in hand, tracing the previous steps of the Piney like it was a trail of honey. The fly marched on with the sun shining brightly down, piercing the pitch pine trees that still stood with burned bark. Nearing the hilltop, the fly was anxious. It was not much of a hill when compared to those in North New Jersey, but one could still feel the rise in their calf muscles as they walked, leaning forward with each step.

After the fly made it to the clearing on top of the hill, he saw, just like the Piney said, the ominous being—the hermit of legend—sitting behind a smoky fire that looked like a tiny log on its side set within a rock ring. As quick as it took the fly's eyes to follow a wisp of smoke from the fire, the hermit was on his feet with his heavy staff in hand. The hermit's green eyes were glowing or maybe illuminated, as if they were catching the sun's rays and radiating warmth; they were not the eyes of fire you would expect if you ever met the Jersey Devil of lore. Regaining a speck of composure, the fly asked, "Umm, hello. Are you the hermit of legend? Can I ask you a few questions?" Like the sound the cedar water makes as it flows out of Oswego Lake, the hermit responded, "No."

"No, you aren't the hermit of legend? Or no, I can't ask you a few questions?" The fly asked. "There's no news here than what you see with your own two beady little eyes, little fly. The land lives on, even with man's inability to control his fire. I am in the mood for only one question, so no, to your child's mind of a thousand questions—just one. You may ask it now but quickly, for I am on my way out."

Seconds turned to minutes before the fly could find the words to meet the giant of a man's demand for just one question. "The Piney whom I lured with honey-laced whiskey told me his granddad said not to hunt in this area of the hill, which was burned to a crisp a few years back. The grandad held the area in high respect and said it was to be protected. He also told me of misplaced shots from a gun that killed neither a magnificent white stag nor you, the hermit, who stands before me this morning. Now, as you tell me, being the fly, I must choose my words wisely and ask only one question of you, who appears to be a living legend or a mythical creature like the headless horseman of Sleepy Hollow. It's an unbelievable demand I must say—but not nearly as unbelievable as you." The fly slyly moved his trigger finger to the camera's button. "I want to ask of you: are you the hermit of legend who is also the great white stag of lore?"

Knowing the answer to his question was irrelevant, the fly took a gamble. He wanted a picture to prove that he had witnessed the hermit, and he knew the hermit, who was in a hurry to go nowhere, would not agree to it. He took his shot at fame and glory. But he failed miserably, as the mighty staff butt hit his head. Echoing in his throbbing head were these words of the hermit and the fading memory of what he looked like. "My staff and my hands, even aged one thousand years, are still quicker than the fly. You asked two questions. You're just like a fly, greedy and selfish, only caring about how much it can eat. A trait in man we hate: gluttony. Still, you found me, one of the guardians of the Pines, and I will answer your questions. Yes, I am one and the same."

15

BRICK BY BRICK ALONG THE CREEK

Summer days are full of adventure when you're all of ten and eleven like cousins Timmy and Willy. This day was no different. The boys were up early, nearly running out the door. Each were yelled at by their mothers to eat breakfast before they run outside, because once they're outside, they disappear for the day, only to resurface at lunchtime and then go right back out to play along the creek again. Any creek provides a lifetime of adventure for any soul who's got a spirit searching for adventure and a heap of fun. And a child's imagination can fill in the gaps to any mystery discovered along the way.

These boys lived only two doors down from each other and less than a mile from Rancocas Creek in New Lisbon, New Jersey.[12] And with a guide who's only eleven years old, they did their best to map out the banks of the creek by foot, starting at the bridge and heading upstream until the sun started to set. It was one of those days when they encountered an abandoned homestead. Timmy, being the youngest and most inquisitive, says, "We must be making good time today and good mileage, as we've never been this far from the bridge. Look at those ruins." Willy, wearing the hat of the sage, blurted, "It's 'cause I didn't let you get distracted at the beginning, and we got in good steps before the bacon was burped out of us from breakfast!" It seems the boys had found an old home located along the creek that time had forgotten. While the boys were fumbling around the area and seeing what could be seen, something caught Willy's eye. He ran over to the water's edge and put his hand up to his brow as he

Above: Canoeing. *Artist, Shane Tomalinas.*

Opposite: Bricks found along Rancocas Creek. *Author's collection.*

strained his eyes to look upstream. Timmy screeched, "Watch your step; it's a snake!" Forgetting what he thought he had seen on the creek, Willy started running. Timmy spotted the snake first, and after Willy got a look, he began reaching for the nearest stick to kill it. Timmy yelled, "No, don't hurt it, Willy! It's good for the environment; remember, we learned about snakes in class with Mr. Anderson just last year."

"Well, you know what Grandpa used to say about snakes. Ain't no good snake unless it's a dead snake," quipped Willy. "Grandpa's dead. And there isn't any wisdom in those words. You know that, Willy." With only one year on Timmy, the healthy-hearted Willy listened to his cousin as much as his cousin listened to him. They made a mighty fine pair. "It's like the house fell down right around itself, and the snake moved in the next day. Look at how black he is. I'm glad we didn't try to kill him," declared the older boy.

As lunch was fast approaching, the boys made their way back to the rendezvous point. Along the way, Willy described to Timmy what he thought was a canoe on the creek, and as the boys hurried along, they kept an eye on the creek to see if anyone was canoeing on this fine summer's day. Willy's mother glanced their way when she heard the screen door slam, and in came the two boys just as she finished making the bologna and cheese sandwiches for the pair. "Mom, we saw a black snake today!" Timmy said, "Yeah, and we discovered an old house, tons of red bricks scattered around an area along the creek." Before Willy's mother could question the boys, Willy told her they did not harm or touch the snake. "That's good, boys. Animals aren't to be trusted no more than humans, and both should be given wide berth and a few ounces of respect, for each of us has the right to life. One more thing about those house ruins: there was a great-uncle in our family tree who disliked people so much, he hauled those bricks down the creek by canoe a mile past where the trail ends. That would be near five miles up the creek. He built his home there in the solitude of the melancholy creek. He took a canoe down the creek every night to get to his little retreat. The sad part of the story is that one night during a bad storm, the creek waters rose so high that they flooded his home. Uncle Sam, asleep in bed, must have been awoken by the water that filled his tiny home. The story goes that after getting out of the house alive, he must have seen that his canoe, along with everything else he possessed, was floating away. When Uncle Sam saw the canoe, he jumped into the creek to save it, but instead, he drowned. They say in the dog days of summer, when heavy rain comes through on the creek, if you're in the right spot, you can catch a glimpse of his ghost canoe, just floating along unmanned, yet steering clear of any overhanging limbs, as if Uncle Sam was at the helm still." The two boys immediately locked eyes but didn't say a word about what they had seen.

16

A WILD CHILD BRINGS THE LIGHT BACK TO THE FURNACE

Ayoung lady, all of twenty-two, sat in the living room window, looking out at Grandma's front yard. Mary Ann had come to Grandma's place to retell the story of an incident that occurred in a place Grandma knew better than most. She hoped Grandma could tell her more. She could not take her story to the police, even though this would have been warranted. Someone of authority had to challenge what she saw and fix what she knew had to be leaking out to the neighborhoods surrounding the military base. Now, she sat in a familiar place, still shaking as the darkness enveloped the objects in the front yard, like Grandma's cement birdbath. Even though she had the knowledge of what the dark shapes were, the scene out the window seemed frightening. Enter Grandma, a Piney of ninety-nine years of age who lived alone at the edge of the woods and Uncle Sam's playground, sandwiched between man and beast.

"Young child, please take this mug of herbal tea to calm your nerves," Grandma said gently. "'Tis true what you saw, for the eyes don't lie. But the mind has a twisted tongue, so you can't believe it when it's spun. I remember bits and pieces of a quote from a book produced by one of the government folks who was out this way in the early 1980s. Let me see where it is." Up on the shelf sat books and knickknacks of all sizes and persuasions. Grandma was a collector of many strange things, and among them were stories, which is why the young lady sought out Grandma's voice. "There it is, a book put out by a lady I met for the first time in the eighties, and years later, I bought this book put out by her in 1994 called *Conserving Culture: A New Discourse on*

Albino Does. *Artist, Shane Tomalinas.*

Heritage." Realizing she was in for a long yarn of Grandma's, the young girl folded her legs in the comfy armed chair. "That young lady's name I forget. Oh, here it is." Grandma pulled down the orange dust-covered book. "It's on the cover—a Mary so and so." Grandma's fingers moved meticulously across the pages, finding the newspaper strip that she used to mark the book, and read aloud, "It is the landscape, rather than a single place, that stores a whole story, preserving individual places without reference to the surrounding landscape; therefore, it is not enough. Nor, for that matter, is the purely physical preservation of the landscape. People must also continue to tell the stories and maintain the practices that make the landscape significant in terms of traditional history. They must be able to keep visiting the places, gathering the materials and performing the ceremonies."

Grandma continued, "My premonition, as I see the state you are in, is that this may serve as an important thread to the story you weave, child, especially since when you first got here, you said it was about Hanover Lake and Hanover Furnace. I remember the meeting as clearly as if it was yesterday; it happened when I turned sixty. That woman, Mary, showed up at my home here in what once was a thriving town of Hanover Furnace. Of course, that was way back in the late 1970s, and I'm happy as pie to still live in this here area that our family's been tied to for generations." Mary Ann interrupted, "Grandma, what's that got to do with me seeing those two deathly white deer that looked like ghosts and less of this world?"

"You see, those educated folks were sent from Washington, direct from the president and Congress even, to see to it that they preserved the people and the Pine Barrens of New Jersey. They saved the latter and forgot all about us. And that's the interesting part of that quote; they're talking about the Navajo people, and what you're talking about is a legend of the local Native Americans, the Lenape. They sent a team out to our area of the Pines to try to save it and us and disregarded the 'us' part of it and put up fences and signs telling us where we could and couldn't go." Grandma shook her hand at the now steady young lady who was seated in her dimly lit living room. "You ignored their signs and went behind enemy lines. Tell me again what you saw."

As most kids do when they live in a rural area, Mary Ann ran out of things to do. She was a Piney girl and one with a keen sense of direction who loved to explore past what the guided tours showed you. Heck, she was named after an old bog iron forge in Browns Mills, New Jersey. To find it, you must have a good sense of direction and a bit of courage to venture out in the Pines, especially alone, as Mary Ann was apt to do. It's said the Jersey

Devil lives in the Pines. Mary Ann gave no mind to these legends and lore and explored even more. It was on such an occasion that she dared to go past the government signs that forbade her entry to a place that had always intrigued her. She had heard stories of this location all her life growing up in the area and while living off and on with her dear old grandmother in the vicinity of a ghost town called Hanover Furnace. But she was always warned to not go into Hanover Furnace—not because the law would catch her but because the area was dangerous. Her grandmother had always left out what would get you if you entered the forbidden area, and it made it even more irresistible to a girl whose name practically spelled adventure.

"I'd been wandering near Whitesbogs, hiking through the woods, when I crossed Range Road and thought I heard a bird that I had never seen or heard before. I know it sounds like a dumb reason to disobey your warnings, but it was like I was entranced by the loud rising and falling sound of its call. Range Road was dead when I crossed it, which might have been my first clue as to what would occur shortly after. I heard the call over and over, like a beacon. With night closing in, I rushed past the Hanover Furnace sign, disregarding the federal red print, and headed north on the trail. The air there seems ancient and mystical. Weird, right?" When Mary Ann looked over at Grandma, she saw in her eyes hints of a tear, and she had a faraway look about her. Grandma did not answer, so Mary Ann went on. "I could smell the dampness in the air. You know there's a lake back there. Right before I got to the water's edge, there was another federal print sign, which was concerning, for it said, 'Restricted Use Area and Contaminated Water.' The funny part—now that I'm telling the story again—is that I remember the bird call stopped when I got to the clearing of the old lake. I scanned the lake area, knowing how little time was left in the day, for I could see the beautiful sun's rays cutting lower and lower on the pitch pines that crowded the lake's shores in all directions. Across the way, toward the east part of the ancient lake, was another clearing."

Mary Ann continued, "There was a short footbridge I had to cross to get near the other clearing, so I walked that way. As I crossed the creek that drained out of the lake, I could see it was covered in a white film of muck. There were still wonderful, lush green plants all around the lake. And I wondered how anything could live, let alone thrive, in this part of the Pines. Eerily though, I never saw a bird near that water. After checking out the wildflowers that were in bloom, especially a patch of orange fringed orchids the size of your patio walkway out front, I turned to head back from where I came. And low and behold, just two steps in and thirty yards

A glowing unknown substance at the bottom of a creek. *Author's collection.*

away, I saw what appeared to me to be two stark white deer. They had no horns from what I could tell, yet they might have had horns, for the sun was setting, and every minute I waited, the closer it got to being completely dark. I watched them for a few minutes, but it felt like an eternity. The third step I took forward came down awkwardly, and even though it was just a small twig I stepped on, it was so quiet, surely anything and anyone could hear a pin drop in that strange silence. Their eyes shot up and looked directly at me." Her grandmother had come back to herself, and now, she was fully aware of the child in her living room, telling a tale she had herself lived many moons ago. She could see Mary Ann was starting to tremble as she relived the terrifying meeting of the infamous pair of ghost deer.

Mary Ann kept spinning her tale. "When their eyes met my own, I was filled with a sense of foreboding—like nothing I had ever felt before. All at once, I understood what they were and felt their hearts beat in mine. For too long, they had been spirits, running along forbidden trails on land closed off by government fences and warning signs, hoping and wishing that one day, a hunter would stalk them and take their lives, thus ending their tormented lives in a cage. The cage was what was once called Hanover Furnace. Long ago, it was a thriving human village, a place of both work and play. Even back then, the deer could move freely, playing a game of catch-me. They had fond memories of stealing into the village gardens and eating fresh corn and tasty yet pretty flowers. Now, they sipped the sludge of Hanover Lake, tasting the poison that was dumped by the man who printed the federal warning signs. Grandma, do you know what happened next?"

An eagerness that Mary Ann hadn't been seen on Grandma's face for decades appeared. And she said, "Yes, child, please, please tell me the rest of the story." After a short pause, not long enough to contemplate Grandma's reaction Mary Ann continued, "After that pin dropped and we connected through a thirty-yard gaze, I felt at one with those two ghosts. Whereas before, I was afraid of what I saw, worried about the dimming of the sun, I was now in a spirit that is hard to describe. My brain was past reasoning of what I was seeing with my own two eyes, and my heart was leading. I stood taller than ever before, and I felt stronger than twenty men. Without knowing it, I closed the thirty yards between me and those two tortured souls in no time flat, and I reached out a hand to each as I stood between them both. My hands were resting on their ghostly necks. It was then that they looked up at me. In a flash, their white coats turned fawn red. I was not at all astonished by their change, but I did recoil my hands from their necks, hovering a few inches away. It was as if I knew what I had to do—my actions would correct a past wrong. For one lonely moment, we just were. In the blink of an eye, they each turned their cheeks higher, soulfully looking me in the eye one at a time, and then they licked the palms of my hands. And just like that, they disappeared. At that moment, the last ray of sunlight was extinguished by the Pines, leaving me in the pitch dark, but in that darkness, my spirit shined so bright, I did not need the sun's beams to guide me out of Hanover Furnace." There ended Mary Ann's tale, and she sat as quiet as a mouse, looking at her grandmother.

Grandma sat with tears rolling down her cheeks. Her tears weren't from fear but elation. She walked over to the sitting Mary Ann and took the child's hands in hers. She rolled over Mary Ann's hands to bear witness to the wild child's kissed palms, "Oh, blessed be, child. You have completed a task I was not up to so many years ago. I did not tell you earlier and I did not tell that D.C. reporter way back then of my own encounter with the two white does."

Grandma continued, "And it has haunted me ever since. There is a popular story of a white stag who comes unannounced—but when he is needed—to a place farther south in the Pines near a bridge. He is a harbinger of faith, for his appearance wards against evil to men. Lessor known is the story of the white does, which lends to the superstition that it is bad luck to shoot any of the albino deer in this area. All stories have a thread of truth to them.

Part I: Albino doe of Browns Mills, New Jersey. *Author's collection.*

Part II: Albino doe of Browns Mills, New Jersey. *Author's collection.*

This, in my ninety-nine years spent on Earth, I have found to be true. I do not doubt any part of your story, for your body tells me all that I need to know. But let me tell you why I sob so. You see, back when I was a young sprout of sixty years, right before I was first introduced to a young lady named Mary from the government, I had done as you did and broken the law, trespassing on what is now government land. I was a bit more foolish, for I wasn't called to the area as you were lured by the bird, but I had told myself for a number of years that it wasn't fair that the government had taken Hanover Lake away from us Pineys. It was my birthright, our family's home. So, I wandered, as you did, past the government fence and government signs in the early evening near the same time—as you have described. But when I got to the footbridge, as you did, my mind would not let me forget nor ignore the warning signs from before. I was deathly afraid of the contaminated water, knowing the government had experimented with war toys and war cannot be contained. So, my mind had deduced the sludge on the water was a toxic byproduct from the rage of men. As the sun was setting, I made up my mind to turn around at once. Then two white does appeared in the clearing, nearly twenty or thirty yards from where I was standing. And do you know what I did? I turned tail and ran home, never looking back!"

Mary Ann asked Grandma, "Why are you shedding tears now, Grandma?" Smiling and wiping her tears, Grandma replied, "It is clear to me now why those two white and ghostly deer appeared thirty-eight years ago. As you described it, Mary Ann, they were tortured spirits wandering the Pines. Their spirits had been poisoned by man's rage, as I had expected, trapping them in a cage we Pineys once called home. The Lenape were here before the Pineys. They were the original caretakers of the land and all that grew on it. One does not possess land; it possesses you. The Lenape knew this. We Pineys learned this early on, but over time, we have lost our way. By the time I had encountered those two hurting spirits, I was too far gone. It was your kindred spirit that spoke to those two ghosts. You, in all your natural beauty and wild, untamed heart, were able to close the gap of our lost ways and bring love back to a dark place. For that, child, you will be remembered as the one who brought the light back to Hanover Furnace!"

17

DO BETTER, SWEET CHILD

As the sun sets, it signals the end of a day, yet many never get to see the sunset of today, as their lives are lost abruptly—they are not really lost but taken by an apex predator, one whose true motives are known only to the devil. The pending police investigation reveals the motives and desires of the assailant. All of their motives are rooted in insanity and never justified. Once taken, a life can never be given back. And the politicization of a death or thousands of deaths is rooted in the same insanity as the actions of the killer. These sentiments can be felt around the world, like the sound of a gun being fired and hitting its target. We all know—and some ignore—the fact that our fellow man can choose to give birth or take life. Yet you and I need only to be alive to become the next victim. For the dead, at least there's peace from the fear of our fellow man.

A little boy is on the street, stomping his feet as if he was stamping out a fire. Nearby, an old woman sees the scene unfolding. At her table outside the café, she asks, "What are you doing, little boy?" The boy looks up and ashamedly responds, "Stepping on these mean ants before they hurt someone." The woman says, "Come over here to me, please." The boy hastily walks over, hoping the woman doesn't cause a fuss; his mother owns the café, and he doesn't want her to find out he's gotten into trouble. Eye to eye now with the older woman, the boy watches as she reaches out to him and pinches his arm. "Ouch! That hurt. Why did you do that?" As the skin of the little boy turns red from the stern pinch, the woman asks, "I do not know you, but I do know those ants that you just killed were my friends." Well, now the little boy's mind is spinning; he's less ashamed and angrier, and he blurts out, "You don't know those ants! And it's not right to pinch me because of what I did to them." The woman responds, "I see. So, it was OK for you to harm them to protect someone else, but it is not OK for me to harm you because they were my friends." Now, feeling like he is on the winning side of the argument, the boy demands, "If I was to tell my mom you pinched me, she would be mad at you, for you're bigger and older than me! You should say you're sorry to me." Sipping her cup of tea and taking a moment to reply to the little boy's demands, the woman states, "You are partly correct. Your mom would be mad that you stood

Ants and Chocolate Chips. *Artist, Shane Tomalinas.*

stomping a hill of innocent ants in the street. Ants and little boys have a lot in common. They both can be harmed by things that are bigger than them. And harm comes from many different places, but the harm that man gives away freely is not from his heart but from his fear of life. The ant isn't mean; it just wants to live."

"She's crazy and a mean old lady. I'm not afraid of ants," thought the little boy. "Then why did I harm the ants? I said that I stepped on them to prevent them from harming others." Just then, the boy's mother comes out the door of the café and, without looking at the boy, asks, "Ma'am, would you like anything else?" Shyly giving the little boy a glance, the woman states, "Yes, please. Could I have four chocolate chip cookies?" The boy's mother replies, "Of course. Be right back." The little boy's mother brings out the plate filled with cookies and departs, leaving the two alone again. "I regret that I ordered too many cookies and can eat only one. Little boy, would you like to help me eat my chocolate chip cookies?" The little boy thinks to himself, "Maybe the little old woman isn't so mean after all." As he's eating the cookies with his newfound friend, the boy concludes, "If I knew they were your friends, I would not have harmed them. I now regret that I stepped on the ants. I'm sorry." Frowning, the old lady says, "In life, unlike ordering too many chocolate chip cookies, regret comes too late. Once you take a life, you cannot give it back. Regret does little to fix things. I ordered too many cookies and could not send them back, but I could share them with you. After a man takes a life—no matter how big or small—what is there left for the man to share with you and me?" Quizzically, the little boy looks at his new friend as he eats cookie after chocolatey cookie.

18

"RIDICULOUS AND INCREDULOUS."

A well-read young man of ten nearing eleven spit out these words as his gaze was fixed on a book: "Ridiculous and incredulous." He had recently returned from a visit with his great-grandmother, who lived in the country. Now back in his suburban home, he sat transfixed by his new book from his great-grandmother, whom he affectionately called Granny. On loan to him was a rare book that was printed in 1907; it was a collection of short stories full of adventure, and it was especially thrilling for this wheelchair-bound young man. The first thing the boy did once he was back home was cozy up to his desk, where he had, numerous times before, ferociously devoured book after book on fishing, hiking and all other outdoor explorations. There, he could tear through the pages—at least metaphorically, for it was his promise to keep Granny's loaned books as clean and serviceable as the day they left her library shelf. After the boy was taken in by a certain chapter in his new treasure, his hunger was fed as fast as his fingers sped across the thick-paged tome. Then suddenly, the story hit a roadblock.

There, on page 281, the print factory had botched the job. Pages 281 and 284 were uncut, so you could not read pages 282 or 283. And again, this travesty was repeated on page 285. When the boy finished the last sentence on this page, the next page was denied him by another uncut page—it kept him from reading pages 286 and 287. Of course, the short story titled "Leviathan" was just getting started, but the lead-ups to the climaxes of these stories always had a few juicy nuggets in them. The boy yelled for his mother, and the only advice she could give him was to call his great-

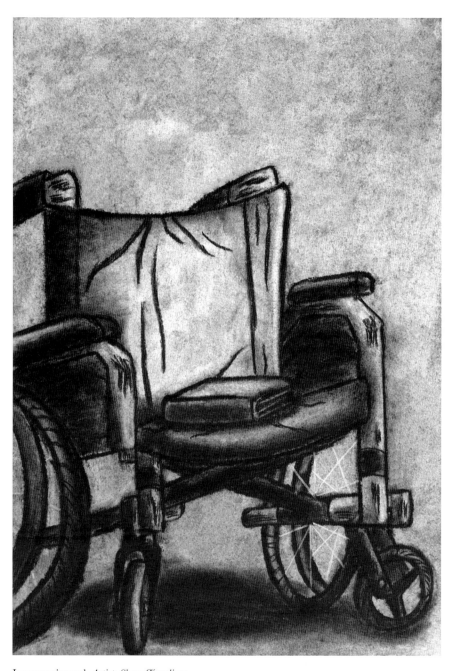

Inconvenienced. *Artist, Shane Tomalinas.*

The folds of the edge of pages uncut. *Author's collection.*

grandmother to see if he could cut the pages. After all, she had lent him the book. "It's not too late now. Can I call her, Mother?" With permission and help, his mother handed him the phone.

On the first ring, Granny answered the telephone with a simple, "Yes. Can I help you?"

"Hi, Granny. I'm calling regarding the book of short stories you sent home with me," he answered. "You see—which, now that I ask, I wonder if you noticed before—that some of the pages are stuck together in the book *Days Off and Other Digressions* by Henry Van Dyke? I would like permission to cut the pages so that I can finish the story." The boy's great-grandmother answered his question with a simple statement: "It's a detour." Her response came quickly and confidently, as if she had anticipated the boy's call. "Where you see a deformity, I see an opportunity, a chance to gain a different perspective. Sure, sure it would be great to be able to read the story as someone with a normal copy of the book can, but normal is boring. The fact it has survived all this time with no one ever being so cruel as to cut the pages is, in itself, a miracle, making it all that more of a rare find. It's extremely rare indeed! As it is, many would conform to the standards of uniformity and be done with it, thus taking what is rare and unique and turning it into something mundane and the same. You, young man, should be acutely aware of this type of judgmental thinking and do your best to avoid it in the future." The boy whimpered, "But Granny, the writer is outlining the differences between the two antagonists, and I cannot see what they are or how this will tie to the rest of the story."

Granny countered, "My father gave me the book in question and hundreds of other first-edition novels when he passed to me the family library, as I will do for you one day. When he did so, he also told me something very important that I've never forgotten. I'll pass that wisdom on to you now, just as I have been loaning you those same books that will be yours one day soon. He said to me, 'These are a collection of true stories from the greatest writers of my time. These stories are true to them. Our family's story continues to be written as each descendant is born. It is up to you to write the beginning, the middle and the end. My father's father's story may have a page torn out, and the ink has probably started to fade on a page or two, yet it's your lifeblood and breath that will write it anew. Their stories of truth are amusing to you and me today. They are remembrances of days gone by, for sure, but the greatest story is yet to be written—it is your own. Each chapter starts with a blank page. Fill it with something worthy of a first edition, to sit on the shelf with the other great novels of old, adding to our family library.'" Granny's words resonated with the boy in a wheelchair. "I see, Granny. Your father told you and you're now telling me that it's our own story that needs to be written by us. In doing so, we continue to grow the family tree. What accomplishments or lack of fortune they may have suffered reflects little on us, for we fill the blank pages with our own truths. And my truth is not limited by the chair I must use to take life's detours." The boy exclaimed, "Oh, and what looks to be a roadblock in life is really just an unwritten part of my story!" The boy's mother, with a tear in her eye, looked down at the boy in the wheelchair as Granny pronounced, "You've got it, kid. Be the first edition you're meant to be. Have a great night."

19

THE GENIUS
OF BLUEBERRY PICKING

It's truly the early bird that gets the worm when it comes to getting to the blueberry patch. Earlier is better if you hope to beat out competing pickers and the summer heat. At the starting line, men, women and children are all outfitted with tin cans tied with strings around their waists. As the whistle blows, the race—or game—is on. Wait a minute—that's all wrong. It's not the best way to describe blueberry picking as some form of sport. For many, it's a tradition that extends through the ages, like celebrating our national holidays. And it's not a competition but a way of life.

Pickers arrive at the blueberry fields early in the morning to get ahead of the heat. But some don't beat it, as the berry season lasts well into the dog days of summer. Still, with the early morning sun glistening on those blue sapphires, people of all ages with tiny pails on strings get to work. Some march to the back of the field, while others walk down the row long enough to find a spot where the berries are heavy on the bush; they then can work themselves back to the beginning. The drumming of the first few berries landing in the bottom of the pickers' near-empty cans is heard over the fields like the tapping in the song "Little Drummer Boy." It quickly deafens as the pickers' hands meticulously search the branches for those shiny blue gems. If they're lucky, the pickers have a full bush in front of them that no one else— except for the thieving robin or a noisy catbird—has picked. The bush, with more limbs than an octopus, is loaded down with the weight of America's favorite fruit. The farmers watch from afar as the pickers do their thing. During the process, the farmer learns a bit about people's personality

Life of a Blueberry. *Artist, Shane Tomalinas.*

types. Some pickers choose only the largest of the berries on the bush and wind up walking for miles up and down the rows before their pails are full. Then there are a handful of pickers who will eat more than they plan on buying. And the farmers' favorites are the professionals. These pickers are sometimes known as "jammers" or "canners," for they preserve wondrous concoctions of fruits in blueberry jams. This blueberry jam or blueberry sauce can be poured over vanilla ice cream—heaven in a bowl on Earth.

The repetitive movement of the pickers' hands is soothing to one's soul, and the food from the blueberry bush nourishes the body. Both the farmer and blueberry picker work in concert to bring these two constructs together in one great sympathy called the blueberry picking season. One may find a pair of siblings in the patch, racing each other to see who can fill their blueberry cans first, but for the most part, this is not the goal. Baseball may be one of our nation's favorite pastimes, but if you live in blueberry country, like New Jersey, you know of another family pastime: the time-honored tradition of going with elders to visit the local blueberry patches. As they say, "many hands lighten the load." At the end of the day, the haul is a national and state blue treasure. It's a tradition, not a sport, for one does it all their life unless they move away from a blueberry state. Life lessons abound in the berry patch, too. A wise old blueberry picker knows the next bush is no bluer than the one in front of you. And you're a darn fool if you keep moving from bush to bush, seeking only large blueberries. You pick the bush clean of all the ripe berries and then move on to the next. And the smaller berries have a tarter and tastier flavor when mixed with a few of the quarter-sized blueberries. And lastly, even dear ole grandma knows that you make sure the farmer has their back turned before you raise your hand to your mouth and stuff it full of blue Jersey goodness!

20

ACCEPTANCE OF CHANGE IS HARD, NO? ESPECIALLY WHEN IT IS DRAMATIC?

An old and wise friend once told me this story, and I am going to share it with you here. The story began one spring, when I watched a newly fledged blue jay come to my birdfeeders in my backyard. From my kitchen window, I could see the scene while watching the television in the living room. It was wonderful to watch the bird's feathers go from drab to sky blue. In a subtle way, before my very eyes, I could see the bird was growing up. Next to the feeders, where the blue jay and other birds sat and ate, there was my native flower garden, which had milkweed plants among other native garden varieties. Each day, the blue jay would retreat to the tall milkweed patch in the garden and eat the seeds from the tray. I wondered to myself when I first witnessed the bird going into the patch if it would discover that there were monarch caterpillars there, eating and growing right alongside it on their own path in life. Then, one day, I heard the bird sounding its jay call: "Jay jay jay!" It seemed the blue jay had discovered a caterpillar and made friends. The bird would land on the tallest milkweed plant in the patch and chatter away while, just below its feet, a yellow-white-and-black-striped caterpillar munched away on a leaf.

Oddly enough, I witnessed this scene play out over and over through my window, which was always better than watching whatever was on the television. Days went by in which the young blue jay would come to our feeders get a birdseed treat and take flight to that same milkweed plant to chat with its newfound monarch caterpillar friend. The monarch caterpillar went through its own growing phases over the time of their

Obnoxious Blue Jay. *Artist, Shane Tomalinas.*

budding friendship. It went from being a tiny thing to a big ole fat cat of a caterpillar. And soon, like the other caterpillars, it finally went into a chrysalis. And one day, that is what the young blue jay found. Nowhere to be seen was its little striped friend, but on the very plant where he stood, inches below one of the leaves, was a shiny green chrysalis. Days went by, and the young blue jay continued as before, grabbing birdseed here and there and landing in the milkweed patch to sound off, as if calling to his long-lost friend. Then, one day, the squiggle squirt of a monarch caterpillar did an amazing magic trick and crawled out of that chrysalis as a black-and-orange-winged monarch butterfly.

It just so happened that as the young monarch was about to take its first flight into the heavens and leave behind its childhood home, the young blue jay was sitting at the birdfeeder. As the once landbound creature took a wondrous leap of faith, spreading its beautiful wings to fly, it took to the sky. I was overjoyed, for I had watched the entire metamorphosis. It seemed to take a long time, but really, it took only days and weeks, not years. And to witness its first flight was a treasure. At the time, I had not thought about how its friend the blue jay would react to the transformation, but in hindsight, if I had thought about it, I would have thought the blue jay would welcome and encourage its butterfly friend and that together, they would fly off into the sunset.

But alas, not all fairytales have happy endings. After only a few seconds of flight, the caterpillar turned monarch butterfly was pierced by none other than the young blue jay's bill. Its hopes and dreams of another life after making dramatic changes were dashed. Had the blue jay not realized it was his old friend in the sky? We suppose because of the blue jay's youth, it was not wise to the fact that the taste of a monarch butterfly is bitter and slightly poisonous due to the white sap of the milkweed. Or could the blue jay not tolerate the changes its friend had gone through, thus changing their friendship? To the blue jay, it was the one who could fly in their friendship. And now that its friend had grown wings, the paradigm had shifted. It was too much, for the monarch butterfly was heading for the sky, leaving behind its old friend the blue jay. And the blue jay was hurt, distraught and mad at the caterpillar for changing. One thing is certain: the blue jay displayed its own immaturity and ignorance by killing his only friend in the milkweed patch, for the blue jay had gone through gradual changes during their friendship, too. It went from an oddly puffy, feathered bird to an adult with a sleek blue suit. Its changes were not as dramatic as being a caterpillar one day and a winged butterfly the next, but nonetheless, the caterpillar wasn't

A blue jay feather. *Author's collection.*

the only one who had changed in the relationship. And yet, the caterpillar was more accepting of its friend's changes and was less envious. The window voyeur stopped watching and paying attention to the young blue jay after that scene played out like a dramatic movie on the old television. So, we'll never know if the blue jay ever expressed remorse or guilt for harming its only friend in the milkweed patch.

Sometimes, even without realizing it, you go through some amazing chrysalis-like growth. And the people around you react differently. Some accept it, some are envious and others refuse to accept it. Think of how many relationships end in divorce because one person does a sudden 180 in their life and they're not the same person the other married. It's sad that we can accept gradual changes, like the graying of our own hair, but when we see a brunette turn blond, we are often unaccepting. This writer, who published his first book in 2021, has felt like the monarch butterfly who is in the sky for the first time right before a friend slams into him and sends him to the ground again. One of the lessons we can take away here is to have harmony in life and to be a good friend. We must know that in either state—caterpillar or butterfly—the changes that occur are sometimes barely noticeable, but at other times, they are dramatic. Still, we must stay the course and support the hopes and dreams of others—to do otherwise would be plain mean.

21

THE TREE AND THE SWING ALONG THE CREEK

Trekking along the creek in the month of April, one has eyes only for the woodland floor. This is because that is where the wildflowers spring up to live their precious, short lives, bravely pushing through the mud-caked banks of the creek to capture sun rays. And when one sees the blankets of spring flowers, one has smiles for miles. It was this type of day that a wildflower photographer was enjoying after walking miles to the natural bluffs along the creek. He had done this season after season, taking snap after snap of pictures worthy of the cover of a magazine. Then out of the blue, the sound of children playing startled him. He took in the forest floor and scanned the horizon, trying to locate the children. It would be odd to find children here, as this spot is a few miles from the nearest home.

The sound was odd to the man, as he had never noticed another person in this area in all the seasons he had bushwhacked to the bluffs. To his knowledge, there was no trail leading along the creek on either side; one just had to battle the briars and follow the deer trails. But where were the children who were laughing so hard that he could hear them way up on the bluffs of the creek? Finally, after ten minutes of motionlessly scanning the creek sides with his hand held over his brow to shield his vision from the bright sunlight, the photographer took up his handy camera and extended the lens to look through the viewfinder. And there, he caught movement down below, on the north side of the creek from where he stood. He could barely make out the two figures who looked like they were swinging from a tree over the creek. He snapped a photograph out of reflex. Then his

Left: Did You See It? *Artist, Shane Tomalinas.*

Below: Crosswicks Creek in Monmouth County, New Jersey. *Author's collection.*

An abandoned swing set over Crosswicks Creek. *Author's collection.*

curiosity got the better of him, and he wanted to get a little closer to see what all the fun was about. So, he headed down the bluffs.

While carefully making his way down the steep gully walls, the photographer heard a piercing wail. He looked up, and as he did so, he fell backward, landing on his butt. In one quick motion, he slid down the rest of the way, landing on the gully floor. Across the north side of the creek, he could see a girl was in the water under the swing, calling to the young boy to save her. The man sat, confused and dumbfounded by his slide down from the bluffs. He watched in horror as the boy jumped into the fast-moving water at the edge of the creek; he was taken under within seconds. The girl's arm shot up to touch the bottom of the green swing, but the man saw only her tiny fingernails scrape the bottom of the seat. Finally jumping to his feet out of shock, the man leaped to rescue the tiny, longhaired girl. But as he got to the edge of the creek, where the tree swing and the two children were playing, the bodies of the two vanished.

The photographer had just heard and seen with his two own eyes two children who couldn't have been more than eight or nine years old playing along the creek. Now, the creek had swept them away, and he was filled with such panic that his heart was racing and his hands were shaking. It all unraveled so quickly. There should be signs of them in distress in the

A simple joy, swinging along the water. *Author's collection.*

water, yet it's like they were never there to begin with. Looking down at his camera, questioning what he had just witnessed, the photographer checked the viewfinder for the image of the two children playing on the green swing set. As he looked at the image, he was once again dumbfounded. Quickly pushing the zoom button on the camera, he looked over the image of the green swing, but there were no children in the image. He thought to himself, "Wait, they were there. I heard their sweet laughter and saw the little girl's last attempt to reach the swing seat." His pulse was racing like a revving car engine. What just happened to this poor man?

Tragic things happen to good people all the time. Some of our lives are swept away before they even begin to grow. The spring wildflowers show us that life is precious and that a lifetime is relative to the destiny that lies ahead. Some of us are wildflowers growing along a creek bank, and others are children swinging gayly in the summer wind. Both are somewhat tragic stories. We can gaze at the wildflowers of spring and wonder why they don't bloom longer. And we can look at the empty green seat and wonder if the course of events occurred as the photographer witnessed or if his imagination got the best of him. Still, the swaying swing in the summer breeze tempts the next child to adventure along the creek. It's another day, and another story is yet to be written.

22

RUINS OF MAN'S FOLLIES

L ook up the word *empath*, and you'll find it's defined as a person who feels empathy for the experiences and feelings of others, like another's pain and happiness is their own. When I look at an abandoned home in the Pinelands or even in my neighborhood, I can't help but feel for those who once lived there. That's why you rarely, if ever, see me capturing images of abandoned homes. I don't feel the curiosity of the spectacle. I feel the pain of those who had to die in order for such a home to turn to ruins. A robust farmhouse gone to ruins means only death. Maybe it was the death of a family name, the death of an individual family member or the death of a vibrant creator who once had a vision. I just don't understand the human curiosity of going into an abandoned home.

Abandoned, man-made structures that were used as tools in life now tell a different story. They are relics of life, ruins of man's follies and accomplishments that litter our landscapes. I place a buffer around my heart when I view an old cranberry pumphouse from afar or up close. I see the four corners of the man-made building and witness the losing battle the roof and man's hands have fought. Moss grows on and around the artificial shelter for a metal mechanism that once controlled water. Witnessing the steel rust does not hurt my heart like seeing a home turn to a pile of dirt. Maybe this is because I know this land was put into preservation intentionally, whereas someone's home does not become abandoned by design.

Lately, my being wants to seek sites full of life—a deep, dark Atlantic cedar swamp; a roadside stand of railroad Annie; and a bog full of redroot.

Time Moves On. *Artist, Shane Tomalinas.*

Abandoned and falling down. *Author's collection.*

I'm just not as interested in the abandoned homes and abandoned towns of our past. At any moment, we could find ourselves in that same predicament. Maybe you are the last of your surname, all of your family having passed on. Now, your empire of dirt will be left behind to wait for the state to consume it. When you see multiple empty homes in your neighborhood, the malaise of our society and our economic problems become reality. Malaise is such an ugly feeling and ugly word. It provokes a feeling of discomfort, knowing there is more to the story than an open door and a rotting roof. I say we should look to the natural life that is in the Pinelands and leave the abandoned homes to future developers.

23

STORY OF THE
OLE MOUNT HOLLY JAIL

J ust a generation before you, the reader, were born, a plethora of amazing stories existed, waiting to be told. If you can get a storyteller to share a tale or two, you'll come away with a handful of family legends brimming with legendary folklore. These events aren't secrets, yet they are stowed away from the scribes of history and certainly are never revealed to academic types. Yet these stories are as important as the battles of the American Revolution in one way or another, for they give delightful details of a time that no longer exists, and each hand-me-down story grows taller every time it's told. Each generational storyteller places emphasis on details that they hold higher value in, whereas the original storyteller may have highlighted other parts of the story. Thus, the legend grows.

How do you get these individuals to share an interesting tale, a story or two that should be written down and shared with the masses? The storyteller crafts the story with bits of truth and feelings of admiration for the characters in the tale. A cloudy memory adds in a bit of creative logic that is shared with a friendly listening ear. That's the key to being witness to these tall tales of old. It's that easy. All you have to do is be a good listener. Have you ever heard of Mount Holly, New Jersey, and its now-closed infamous jailhouse? The following story details a local family's ties to the hard times spent in the Mount Holly Jail. This is the legend of a man who could lift a Farmall tractor so high that the rear tires cleared the ground while they were removed and repaired—like a truck jack.

Left: Justice or Injustice? *Artist, Shane Tomalinas.*

Below: An exterior photograph of the Mount Holly Jail, now the Burlington County Prison Museum. *Dennis McDonald, 2020.*

This story was told around the kitchen table at Joe and Charlotte's house in New Egypt, New Jersey. This author asked, "A friend of mine from the band Jackson Pines sang a song by Merce Ridgeway Jr. about the Mount Holly Jail in 2023. It's an old song about tough times spent in Mount Holly Jail. Pa, I remember that you said something about Uncle Joe Boy spending time there." This presented an opportunity to capture a story of old.

We can't judge the people of the past through the lens of today. As things occur in the present, on-hand experience is taken in as society learns and establishes new norms, and our collective morality changes with the times. This allows us to see history with a new lens, as it were. Americans have a long tradition of overconsuming alcohol—to our detriment. Today, we know the pitfalls of alcoholism. When listening to someone telling stories that occurred in the 1950s, 1960s and 1970s, we sometimes think, with our present lens, that the people then were much more rambunctious than us. Part of the blame for the actions of people then should fall on the spirits found at the bottom of clear and brown bottles. It wasn't unheard of for people then to start their day with a good drink, and those with a weak will would keep drinking the day away—the proverbial ticking bomb or stick in a wasp nest.

Joe replied, "Uncle Joe Boy was in jail there. He spent time because of petty crimes, like stealing. We went down there with Mommy to see him. When was that, Dear?" Joe's wife, Charlotte, added, "He spent quite a few years there. It had to be in the seventies, because we had just gotten married." Joe picked the story back up. "He wasn't the only one we knew who spent time in the Mount Holly Jail. When it happened with Johnny Bowker, my brother Butchy [Wayne Britton (1954–1975)] was a baby. I wasn't even born. Joe Boy spent his time in the jail later."

"Wait," this author interrupted. "If you weren't born, who told you the story?"

Joe replied, "Daddy told me the story, and later, Johnny himself retold it to me. Johnny got in fight with Big Sam, Daddy's brother. Maybe it was his size—he was a big man, six feet–plus—that drew a fight or his short temper, but Johnny was always in a bit of trouble. Daddy witnessed the fight in the house there on Magnolia Road in Pemberton, New Jersey. They had a fight, because, for some reason, Johnny hit Baby Butchy and Big Sam went at him. Johnny was Daddy's cousin, and they worked together doing odd jobs, like junking or cutting pulp wood. Also, they all drank together, but I'm not sure they were drinking this day or not. In the fight, Uncle Sam and Johnny knocked the wood-burning potbelly stove over while the fire was still going.

Wasp's nest. *Author's collection.*

Thankfully, the house didn't go up in smoke. Somebody called the cops, and they took Johnny Bowker away. The funniest part of the story is when Johnny went to court to get sentenced. Johnny didn't believe he should be in trouble at all, and his attitude in front of the judge showed it. When the judge awarded him thirty days in the Mount Holly Jail, he was mad, and he responded to the judge, 'I can do that standing on my head!' He was always too hot-tempered to keep his mouth shut. The judge replied, 'Well I'll give you thirty more days to get back on your feet.'"

Being poor and uneducated, along with having a hot temper and a bit of liquid courage, is a recipe for disaster. It was years later that Johnny Bowker's life circumstances led to another fit of rage. Trouble came knocking again in the form of a crime of passion. No matter how hard Johnny worked—with the strength of Lennie from John Steinbeck's book *Of Mice and Men*—worries with the law troubled his days. He shared a fate with the good-natured character in Steinbeck's book, but instead of winding up on the receiving end of a bullet, he was the one pulling the trigger.

As they are in all good stories, the characters must be pitted against the odds, sometimes playing the villain and, other times, the hero. In this instant, was he the victim of cruel circumstance or the victimizer? He was never an even-tempered man, and he leaned more on the strength of his hand than he did on being a thinking man. In this part of the story, we find our antihero caught up in a love triangle, which eventually led to another day in court. His crime now was more serious than before, but this time, he had a different judge—and better luck.

Continuing the story, Joe said, "Johnny was my dad's cousin, but near everyone in the family had at least one story of being angry with him or wanting to fight him, regardless of the size of the man. He was the biggest man you've ever seen. I watched him lift a Farmall tractor by grabbing the rear drawbar and raising the tires off the ground."

This author interjected, "It seems Johnny was a magnet for trouble."

Joe nodded and continued the story. "Over on Millstream Road in New Egypt, my cousin Brenda lived, and even though there was a big gap between their ages, Johnny and Brenda were romantically involved. They rented a home together, being common-law partners, from Mrs. Lovee, an African American woman who owned the home but didn't live in town anymore. A guy the same age as me at the time—because we went to school together—Charlie Binn, in his twenties, and another friend were hanging out at the

Part I: a jail cell's lock in present-day Burlington County Prison Museum, also known as the Mount Holly Jail. *Dennis McDonald, 2020.*

Part II: a jail cell's open door in present-day Burlington County Prison Museum, also known as Mount Holly Jail. *Dennis McDonald, 2020.*

house there with Brenda and some say were up to no good. Johnny wasn't at home either but was expected any minute, and the story goes that the other guy was trying to get Charlie to leave before Johnny got home. However it played out, it's said Johnny shot Charlie Binn and was arrested for it; this was in the 1970s. In his defense, Johnny said it was in self-defense, as Charlie wouldn't leave the premises. That didn't mean that someone should be shot and killed. Whatever the reason—maybe there was a lack of witnesses and it was one person's word against another—but this time, Johnny was saved from a trip to Mount Holly Jail. Even though he got arrested and was charged with killing Charlie Binn when he went to court, he got off."

The lyrics of the song "Mount Holly Jail" sung by Jackson Pines go something like this: "It's hard times in the Mount Holly Jail / It's hard times in the Mount Holly Jail / Hard, hard, times." Sometimes, a grim four-walled cell becomes the only setting for someone who repeatedly winds up on the wrong end of the law. Unlike George and Lennie's actions in this story, in John Steinbeck's book *Of Mice and Men*, Lennie's actions were never done to intentionally hurt anyone—whether mouse or woman. The only real comparison is that trouble easily found both Johnny and Lennie. And the hurt from their actions didn't just affect their victims. You can judge whether the story is fiction or fact, but remember, conflicts are hard-fought in a courtroom when the only answer is at the end of a dark hallway in a four-walled room. The Mount Holly Jail had a reputation for being a place where the only thing that could grow was mold on the food and lice in the prisoners' hair. If we're looking to truly reform and reinvent our lost citizens, where's the light in that setting?

24

THE HISTORY OF EMERY'S BERRY PATCH AND BEYOND

How far have we come in the Northeast—and probably across the entire United States? Once, small towns provided the strength to harvest what farmers planted in rows, but today, it's supermarkets that brings us "fresh produce." Early pioneers of the farming industry are forgotten today as we worry whether the fruit is organic or not. And forget about how far the soil and the farmers have come since early days. In the early 1940s—not that long ago—nearly every American had a victory garden that they used to help feed their family, and communities were built around dairy farms and vegetable farms. Communities provided the manpower needed to supplement the farmers' inherent workforce (i.e., daughters and sons). The phrase "many hands lighten the load" rings a bell. Did you know that much of the brute strength put into the farming industry was given to earn just enough money to buy school clothes? In this story, we will explore the days gone by, just one or two generations ago, when times seemed simpler and, in this case, sweeter. No longer is our society agrarian in nature, but the inspiring life stories of old can still provide us with much inspiration in a technological society.

Mrs. Gail Miller (née South, age seventy-four) remembers those days fondly.

Now, it's been sixty years, give or take, but I remember riding my bicycle from 10 Terrace Avenue, New Egypt, New Jersey, to Grandmom and Grandpop's about three miles out to Cranberry Canners Road in the summer

U-Pick Blueberry Time. *Artist, Shane Tomalinas.*

to join them in picking blueberries. My whole life was spent in a three-mile radius of home. Seems that blueberries today start earlier, as I remember it being around Fourth of July when all of us kids were out of school and everyone you knew from the community—both kids and adults—picked blueberries in the summer. Most kids my age that I knew would pick for Emery's Blueberry Farm on Long Swamp Road in New Egypt. Part of me was like, "Aww. I wish I was up there with the other school kids." But the other part of me was glad to be spending the day with my grandparents. All through middle school, we picked. At that age, I probably ate a lot of berries, but we worked hard picking, too.

Blueberry and cranberry culture runs deep in southern New Jersey. There are many stories of locals picking berries in the summer and scooping cranberries in the fall. It was an annual thing that the local community all participated in. It was also another way to earn extra income—a means to an end, as they say. Middle school children even participated in the workforce to earn money for back-to-school clothing or a new bike. Emery's farm sent a truck to local towns to pick up the school-aged children and others who wanted to pick for the day and would return them to their towns when the day was done. Mrs. Gail Miller was the youngest berry picker at the Cranberry Canners Road operation, as they employed mostly adult workers, like Gail's grandfather Clifford J. South, who lived on the same street and owned a three thousand–plus chicken farm. He farmed corn on both sides of the road, and Mr. Enoch Bills's bogs and berry patch were on the eastern side of the road, set back a way. Gail recalled how her grandfather would go into town to visit one of the several mills (maybe the one on Province Line Road, now across from the Catholic church), Mr. and Mrs. Roger Atkinson's place (1938–58); there Grandpa would take his corn to get ground and have it turned into chicken feed. Gail says, "It takes a lot of feed to keep all those hungry birds happy. And if you stop laying eggs, you become supper." Like other residents, Mr. South supplemented his income by helping the neighbors with scooping cranberries and picking those sapphire gems known as blueberries for Mr. Enoch Bills. In this period, harvesting was strictly powered by the local population.

Mrs. Miller continued.

Mr. Enoch Bills owned the cranberry operation and blueberries. He had two site managers, Edna and Winifred "Winnie" Grant, who supervised the berry picking. They would shout, "Mr. Bill's coming! Mr. Bill's

Red-ripe cranberries. *Author's collection.*

coming!" So, everyone needed to be busy picking. You didn't pick the green ones, but you were sure to pick the berry bush clean. Any berries you left behind were lost money. With a metal can tied around your waist and a wooden carrier, that's how'd you spend your day. The handmade wooden carrier held twelve-pint boxes; when you got it filled, you yelled, "Carrier! Carrier!" They'd come, take the full one and bring you back an empty one. You'd also get a hole punch to your paper ticket when you got a carrier full, and that's how you got paid at the end of the day, tallying up how many times your ticket or tickets were punched.

Author Dorothy S. Mount, in 1979 book titled *A Story of New Egypt and Plumsted Township*, wrote, "A road that leads to the house where the first cranberry jelly was made. Mrs. Lee and her nephew, Enoch Bills, were owners of vast cranberry bogs. Whether Mrs. Lee started making jelly as a hobby or envisioned a market for their berry crop, is anyone's conjecture, but start she did on the range in her kitchen with the help of Mrs. King, Mrs. King's children, and other neighbors." Mrs. Elizbeth Lee was known to be the first person to can cranberry sauce under the label Bog Sweet in New Egypt, New Jersey, in 1917, eventually going on to be part of the founding of Ocean Spray. Both of her parents had emigrated from Ireland. Widowed, she turned to her sister's son, structural engineer Enoch Bills, to help with the cranberry canning operation in the early 1930s. The siblings were known less for their blueberry business and more for their trailblazing in the cranberry industry at Cranberry Canners Plant No. 3. Later, the property was sold to Mark Havey before it more recently became a public open space and nature park. About five miles east on Long Swamp Road, another first took place in the same relative timeframe, continuing the story of those tiny blue sapphires that America and the world have grown to love.

But first, who brought us the modern-day blueberry? The cranberry industry is the elder brother of the blueberry industry in southern New Jersey. But usually, where you find cranberries, you can also find wild huckleberries, which, with a little bit of help the blueberry bush, eventually blossomed to have an industry all its own, another opportunity for farming in the sandy, barren landscape and swampy soil. Round and deliciously sweet, the blueberry of today and its story of cultivation is credited to Mrs. Elizabeth Coleman White at her family's cranberry farm Whitesbog in Browns Mills, New Jersey, and Frederick Coville, who was a USDA botanist in 1916. This pioneering enterprise between the two of them led to the blueberry culture of today and spread like wildfire across the region, with blueberry patches being planted in swampy areas next to cranberry bogs, like Elizabeth Lee's and Enoch Bills's patches on Cranberry Canners Road. And this effort wouldn't have been as fruitful as it was without the paid assistance of the local woodsmen, or Pineys, who brought Mrs. White the best and biggest berry-producing wild huckleberry plants.

Just ten miles as the crow flies northeast of Whitesbog Village and Cranberry Farm and only five miles east of Enoch Bills's Berry Patch and the canning factory for Bog Sweet cranberry sauce was the setting for another first. This is where a pioneer and self-proclaimed Piney lived and, through necessity, changed the face of blueberry picking in the region: 346 Long Swamp Road in New Egypt, New Jersey. At the time, this industry was yet to develop fruit, but today, it is as bountiful as traditional farming and has blossomed into an industry known as agritourism. Today, you can pick your own vegetables and fruits across the fruited plain of America— everything from purple lavender, garden-variety vegetables, ruby-red cranberries and, of course, those highly sought-after blue sapphires, or blueberries.

Back in the early days of farming, this was unheard of. After World War I, laborers were hard to find, and farm owners turned to local migrant populations for assistance. Whether they were picking ruby-red cranberries or sapphire

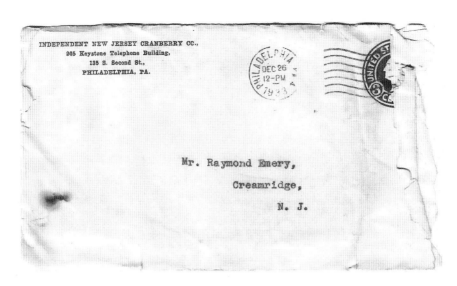

A 1933 postmarked envelope from the Independent New Jersey Cranberry Company, Philadelphia, Pennsylvania. *Courtesy of the Nurko family.*

A 1933 invoice made out to Mr. Raymond Emery from the Independent New Jersey Cranberry Company, Philadelphia, Pennsylvania. *Courtesy of the Nurko family.*

Raymond "Butch" Emery with a huge buck he shot on his property on Long Swamp Road. *Courtesy of the Nurko family.*

blueberries, hundreds of families took part in the industry and were paid by a peck, or a pint. In one sweaty hand, a paper ticket was tallied each day and helped put food on the table and pay the rent. The following are the tales of two different daughters from two men who were lifelong friends. They discuss the history of the Emerys' Blueberry Farm. One was employed by the owner of the first u-pick blueberry operation in the area—and possibly in the nation. The other was the daughter of a tomato and potato farmer who also served as an agent for the Independent New Jersey Cranberry Company, Raymond "Butch" Emery (1909–1975). He later became a blueberry farmer and pioneered the u-pick blueberry practice in 1970. Both of the women's lives and livelihoods were tied directly to what Butch listed on his business card: "Emery's Blueberries— Public Picking—Bring Own Container."

Thelma Davison (née Parker, age eighty-six) said:

> *In 1943, my father, Roy C. Parker, accepted a farming position with Raymond "Butch" Emery, located on the old Joseph Fischer farm* [38 Fischer Road, New Egypt, New Jersey 08533; it had 98 acres and was bought in 1943]. *My family lived there in 1943. We stayed in the house that is Hallock's U-Pick Farm today. Raymond grew tomatoes and potatoes on that farm. Eventually, he fell in love with his future wife, Ida Kotan* [1919–2008], *whom everyone called "Babe." She lived with her family, the Kotans, down the road at another farm on West Colliers Mill Road. They got married and moved into the main house on the farm, but before that, Raymond gave my parents 1.9 acres to build a new house, and the parcel was large enough for a large family garden. Raymond started blueberries in a patch nearby. Mr. and Mrs. Horner were an elderly couple that lived in a house on the righthand side of the road, entered by way of a side, bumpy dirt road that went into the 5-acre blueberry patch* [the blueberry field comprised 5 acres in the Village of Archertown, and he paid $300 for it].
>
> *He was still living at the house on Fischer Road when Raymond and my dad, Roy, would go to New Egypt and pick up young blueberry pickers who were on their summer vacation from school. Elderly people would also pick berries for a few extra dollars back then. Also, the field blueberry pickers would start early in the morning. As a teenager, I worked in the packing shed. The ripe berries picked in quarts were put out on a screened section and sorted so that the bad ones could be removed upon inspection. They were then drained down into a wooden box. They would be graded, and each box weighed twenty-two pounds. We used in-house wooden carriers that Raymond and my father would make in the offseason. Each day, the pickers started with empty cups/pints in those wooden carriers and filled the cups to the top and would then bring them back to us in the shed. They would have a ticket with numbers on it, and the shed workers would punch*

how many pints the workers had picked. Later, we graduated from the pint cup to the quart cups. In the packing shed, we would top off the pints and then use a little gadget that would fit over the top of the pint cup and carefully place a piece of cellophane over the finished pint. We then put elastic around the cellophane pints. The quart cups weren't packaged with cellophane. The pints and quarts had separate custom-made carriers that Raymond and Dad made in the wintertime, when work was slow. They also pruned the blueberry bushes during this time. Raymond would sell the blueberries at the co-op in Hammonton. Eventually, they went from packing in pints and quarts to selling in bulk.

Clara Nurko (née Emery, age seventy-six) remembered:

My dad came from a poor family but was very industrious. He was a vegetable farmer before blueberries. He also sold cranberries in the 1930s, as we have old receipts from Philadelphia. Raymond Emery's name was stamped on them, describing him as an official cranberry broker of the Independent New Jersey Cranberry Company. Records from September 27, 1935, show cranberries of David Foulks appoints Raymond Emery to scoop, pick and harvest half of the cranberries growing on Hartshorn Mill Stream Road, Plumsted, Ocean County. He also made a lot of investments in land, turning a piece of land around when the price went up and making a profit. At one point, he went to North Carolina and bought a blueberry farm with a partner. His partner was Herb Clevenger from Pemberton, New Jersey, and they owned fields together and had separate fields as well in North Carolina. In April, they would travel down to meet with a local person who was hired to maintain the fields year-round. The blueberry picking season pretty much was from the first of July to the end of August in New Jersey. Things would be good money-wise, but if you had a late frost, it could totally wipe out your early crop. And we had years like that— lost money in North Carolina, and we lost money in New Jersey. That is the way farming was and still is today. Hopefully, you had enough set aside that you could make it through. Dad was an avid deer hunter, and we had a freezer stocked with venison. My brother David and I, along with Mom and Dad ate venison year-round. Dinner was always at 5:30 p.m. Two staples of our diet were venison and blueberries. Dad was diabetic. Clara Emery, Raymond's mother, died of blood poisoning, but she really was diabetic, too. Blueberry muffins and blueberry cobbler were always favorites at home. Blueberry pie was good but too much work—time was short. My

Raymond Emery and his five-year-old granddaughter, Christy Nurko Esandrio, in the spring of 1974. *Courtesy of the Nurko family.*

mother said certain blueberry varieties always made better desserts. Varieties that were a little tart made the best ones. Dad did not indulge in desserts, though, because of his diabetics.

Dad only had one fulltime employee and a lifelong friend—not just boss-and-employee relationship—in Thelma's dad, Roy Parker. They did everything together. And Roy did everything on the farm—did the pruning of the bushes and then, in the winter, if they weren't out pruning, they would be making the wooden carriers [two sizes: pint and quart] *that the pickers used. Both were avid deer hunters. A little after I was born in 1947, Dad and Roy planted the farm fields where the current Emery's*

144

Blueberry Farm is over at 346 Long Swamp Road, which is where Emery's blueberry operation moved to in 1953. We still farmed the five acres off Archertown Road in New Egypt. Both of my parents were such hardworking people. Dad never finished elementary school, as he had to work to help his family live. He loved the area, the land, the fresh air, flora and fauna. I remember him picking May pinks in spring in the woods for Mom's kitchen table. Smart, creative and innovative, he was a true Piney and very proud of it. Pineys made do with what they had. I remember Dad was handy, too, because he had to be—not just on the farm, but when they moved to Long Swamp Road, he remodeled the house there. And I remember this old wooden cradle [cherry cradle, circa 1800s] *was found in the attic of an old barn on Fischer Farm from the original property when purchased. Dad cleaned it up and replaced the bottom board and one each of the rockers and spindles before refinishing it. You could tell it was used where the parents foot kept the cradle rocking.*

Resourcefulness and independence were two qualities many farmers had, and farmers relied on the community around them to bring the full bounty of their fruits and vegetables to the market. Today, there are child labor laws with safety precautions put in place to protect our youth. But back in Clara, Thelma and David's day, you worked hard for what you needed, not what you wanted. In an interview in May 2021, Clara Nurko was asked if she considered their family wealthy when she was growing up, as she came from one of the first successful u-pick blueberry operations in southern New Jersey. She responded, "David went to college; I went to a two-year secretarial school. We never had fancy cars or fancy clothes. I picked and packed blueberries, just like anybody else, just so I'd have money to go to Trenton, because that's where you went to buy your clothes. There was only one clothing store in New Egypt. In Trenton at the time, we would go to Arnold Constables, Yards, Lit Brothers and combine it with a movie. The best movie theaters were in Trenton, even though New Egypt had a movie theater of its own." The local children were part of the workforce, too, and not just the farmer's children.

The cranberry and, later, blueberry industries improved with technology. Whereas hundreds of pairs of hands were needed to pick a cranberry bog clean, the invention of the wooden cranberry scoop took the number of helpers down to high double digits, and in the 1950s, with inventions like the Darlington, a cranberry picking machine, only a handful of helpers were needed on the farm during harvest season. But in the blueberry industry,

Christy Nurko Esandrio, Raymond's granddaughter, at age six in July 1975. *Courtesy of the Nurko family.*

where handpicking is the preferred method, humans are much more desired in the fields. Even in Raymond Emery's lifetime, more lucrative jobs, along with restrictions on children in the workforce, took residents out of the work pool. And migrant help was costly or not sufficiently available to pick all the blueberry bushes clean. The *Asbury Park Evening Press*, on Friday, July 30, 1971, reported, "Frustrated by the difficulty of securing efficient help in sufficient quantity, Mr. Emery opened his fields several years ago to the public." Since 1968, Ida and Raymond Emery—and later, their son David—have embraced the new way of getting those blue jewels off the bush: have the public pay you to do it!

TELEPHONE: (609) 758-8514

Emery's Blueberries

Public Picking
BRING OWN CONTAINERS

RAYMOND EMERY

LONG SWAMP ROAD   NEW EGYPT, NEW JERSEY 08533

Above: Emery's public blueberry picking business card. *Courtesy of the Nurko family*.

Left: David Emery and his son Joel during the summer blueberry season of July 1984. *Courtesy of the Nurko family*.

As world events collide, new business ventures become prime for the undertaking. In the aftermath of the Vietnam War, which officially ended in 1975, and the passing of Raymond Emery that July, David (1945–2021) inherited the farm, where he had already been working since his twenties, and continued the family business for ten more years. Eventually, in 1985, he sold the blueberry farm to Dan and Diane Passoff. They, in turn, sold it in 1998 to Mr. Michael and Mrs. Susan Marchese and their son John Marchese, who still run the business under the name Emery's U-Pick Blueberry Farm and Country Bakery. But back when it all began, times were different. Memories of the story of a traditional blueberry farm, with local hired hands, both big and small, are fading. Back then, these workers served as blueberry pickers with tin cans wrapped around their waists, greeting each new day with wide smiles. Hours and hours were spent in the fields until the season came to a blistering end in late August. Everyone earned the much needed income to help sustain their way of life. As times changed, so did farming practices, and innovative workforce solutions were needed. One man revolutionized the blueberry picking field out of necessity; he'd lost a viable local workforce and turned to drastic measures. Trusting they would eat less than they picked and that they would pay him to pick those blue sapphires in the sun, he invited the public to pick their own berries. It was the dawn of a new day and a new industry: ecotourism. How confident were the Emerys in their only option: turn to the people and charge them for the picking pleasure and the ability to take home the shiny, blue and tasty sapphire treats? The morning of the first day of u-pick blueberry season, proprietor and pioneer Raymond Emery summed it up in a rhetorical statement: "What if no one comes?"

25

LEGENDARY HESSIAN ISLAND IN THE PINES

You've probably experienced it yourself. You're sitting around the kitchen table, the youngest in the room, listening to your parents, uncles, aunts and grandparents telling stories that start with, "Remember when?" The talking goes on for hours and hours, and some tall tales go in one ear and out the other, leaving you without a word to remember, but then there are those few tales that sound too cool to be true. The following tall tale comes from a kitchen round table discussion, just as the one described. The grandparents are long gone from this Earth, but they are part of the story as well. How much is truth and how much is fiction? You'll need to be a detective like Nancy Drew or the Hardy Boys to find out, yet facts from colonial times are hard to corroborate, and the more research you do, the more rabbit holes you go down.

Uncle Donald Emery (1955–2020) said, "Dad always called it Hessian Island." His brother-in-law Joe said, "Yeah, your brother Richard [1952–2015] took me there once." This author's mother, Charlotte, excitedly added in, "There's gotta be buried treasure there from when the Pine Robbers used the place for a hideout. Those boys knew the woods better than anyone else." Fast-forward years later, when a trip to explore the area by a father and son resulted in a curious discovery, adding many more questions to the puzzle: Who were the Hessians, and who were the Pine Robbers?

We know Hessians were hired by King George III to fight against the rebellion on the American continent. These roughly thirty thousand German soldiers fought in the American Revolution (1775–83), as did the British

Lost Treasure. *Artist, Shane Tomalinas.*

regular military. Wikipedia notes the use of foreign mercenaries was one of the grievances the colonists listed in the Declaration of Independence in 1776. In local legend appears the name Hessian Island. Tradition says that in Ocean County, New Jersey, there was a band of outlaw Hessians and Tories who, during the American Revolution, lived in secret areas of the Pines, harassing and routinely robbing local stagecoaches, prominent citizens who supported the Patriots and just about everyone they could intimidate and steal from. Other than traveling by foot or on horseback, the only available transportation in our rising nation's rural countryside were manned stagecoach routes.

In New Jersey, these coaches took city folk safely through the Pine Barrens to one of the towns along the Jersey Shore. Inland, away from the privateering enterprise, there was still plunder to be had, for those nefarious characters knew the lay of the land by foot or hoof. This period was full of unrest for the local people of New Jersey. In Monmouth County, especially, neighbors were pitted against each other, and in some instances, families were split between the two warring factions. Formerly New Jersey Volunteers fought opposite the New Jersey Militia, which was made up of Loyalists or Refuges. The former were later known as Patriots and Whigs. It wasn't just Pine Robbers who were marauding through communities and taking items that did not belong to them. The British army's Hessian division(s) were known to ransack villages as they advanced across the New Jersey countryside. It was a time of uncertainty; no one knew who to trust, as mankind has a great ability for deception. One's motives and intentions were just as hard to ascertain then as they are today. The most feared during the American Revolution were the lawless desperadoes, Tory Refugees and "Pine Woods Robbers," who infested old Monmouth County. Today, those same lands, where the banditti hid out in the cedar swamps of the Pine Barrens, are now known as Monmouth and Ocean Counties, established in 1850. And Burlington County had its own share of Pine Robber incidents, as you'll soon discover.

When they were caught stealing and chased by local militia, the Pine Robbers would disappear into thin air. They escaped into the evergreen pines, taking with them their loot. Not all escaped; a few were met with justice after running rampant in the small rural communities of southern New Jersey. Historians have written about a few famous Pine Robbers who ultimately and famously met their ends from a swinging tree branch, a rope around their necks. They were notorious refugees who stole and murdered, regardless of what side of the war their victims were on. Private citizens were targets as long as they had valuable loot or threatened the Pine Robbers' existence in some way. There was a heightened sense of vengeance from the Tory league of banditti, who targeted Loyalist family homesteads and took to the streets with the bravado of "an eye for an eye." This made them all public enemy no.1. Many of the characters in the Tory league of despoilers, like John Bacon, Richard Davenport, William "Bill" Giberson and his lookalike sister and Joseph "Joe" Mulliner have been documented, and their historical footnotes have been written. But there are lesser-known skirmishes with the Pine Robbers that occurred and are now lost to history, waiting to be discovered. In all these stories, one has to ask: Where did all the stolen treasures and the dozens of men who weren't caught and punished disappear to? Maybe their ghosts still haunt the undiscovered and hidden stolen gold and Continental paper currency out in the remote sections of the Pine Barrens of New Jersey.

One cold day in January, Martin Luther King Jr. Day 2020, two people set out to find Hessian Island.

This author says, "We cross the creek single file with Dad in the lead. He curses and goes knee-deep in the creek. He has on better boots than me, with his muck boots on and me with my water-resistant hiking boots." Dad says, "Your uncle Richard did that. When I was here with him ten years or so ago, he fell in, and I didn't."

This author continues, "I advance with caution, using some high-bush blueberry brush to half pull half spring my body across the creek. Dad leads the way, looking for signs of the path he took years ago to find Hessian Island. We wander through the piles of frozen and not so frozen sphagnum moss, leaning on towering cedar trees as we go. The tall Atlantic white cedars are obstructing our view. We turn left, only to turn back to the right as we see a clearing ahead. The *Kalmia latifolia* starts to thicken, and Dad stops. Mind

An overgrown cranberry bog in Colliers Mills Wildlife Management Area, Jackson Township, New Jersey. *Author's collection.*

you, we started late in the afternoon, so the sun is starting to traverse to its resting place, as we've been wandering for a few hours now."

I catch up to Dad, and he says, "Look at that!" There on the rising ground, out of the cedar swamp, is a stone marker. He turns to the other side and brushes the moss clear to reveal the initials "J.B." Dad says, "Well, Richard and I didn't see that last we came through here, but I think we are near the island." Naturally, with an iPhone in hand, I tell Dad, "Wait up, and let me get a few pictures." Dad's not one to linger—you could label him as the "constant impatient one"—so off we go after a few snaps, mindful of the setting sun and having to double back across the Atlantic cedar swamp and the old cranberry bog to exit. Yep, Uncle Richard's ghost probably pushed Dad into that creek knowing he was always an impatient Piney!

There wasn't much to distinguish Hessian Island from any other swamp in southern New Jersey. Southern New Jersey—and the Pine Barrens, in particular—house many ghost towns and many lost industries of the past. Mother Nature takes little time to reclaim what was hers in the first place.

Joseph Lewis standing next to an Atlantic white cedar. *Author's collection.*

Above: Joseph Lewis discovering the mysterious J.B. sandstone marker, January 2020. *Author's collection.*

Opposite: J.B. marker. *Author's collection.*

You could walk right by the ruins of an estate or of a famous paper mill factory and not even know it. Could the newly discovered mysterious marker be a land marker with the owner's initials inscribed on it? Intrigue is what makes history buffs and Pine Barren explorers tick. The key to a lifelong love of adventure is to forever be more curious than a cat. Now, we were trying to run down any leads that would tie this remote area locally known as Hessian Island to past Pineys.

We ran out of daylight that fateful Martin Luther King Jr. Day but found Hessian Island and a mysterious sandstone marker. A return trip to examine the J.B. marker turned up no new clues. We went back, mostly to see if we could find the marker again and confirm that it wasn't a figment of our

imaginations. It was another great day spent in a cedar grove as father and son, but it added nothing to the story of Hessian Island. We even turned to another local explorer and contributor to the *NJPineBarrens* forum, Guy Thompson, to help map out our discovery on state tax maps and try to date the J.B. marker. But our hunt for Hessian Island only added a new mystery

An overgrown and forgotten place in mountain laurel. *Author's collection.*

about who J.B. was, leaving us no closer to solving the mystery of Hessian Island. Where we once had one mystery, we now have two. Maybe we could find something written about the period in question in an old book or two.

A list of names that had the initials J.B. was compiled:

- Joseph Borden (1687–1765): The namesake of Bordentown, New Jersey. Arrived in the area around 1717 and owned a stagecoach line, per the Bordentown Historical Society website.
    › John Borden (1867–unknown, possible son of Joseph Borden): Former mill owner in the area of Borden's Mill Branch. The Borden family owned property included a gristmill before 1768 in same area.
- John Bacon (died 1783): We do not know when he was born or when he turned to villainy.
- Black is a longstanding family surname in the Burlington and Springfield area. In Burlington County, there were several generations of John Black whose initials are J.B. The first John Black came over on the boat *Martha* from Burlington, Yorkshire, England, to settle in Burlington County. Then a grandson named John Black was born in 1752 and became a general of a militia and owned land in Springfield, as noted in the 1883 book *History of Burlington County New Jersey*, by Major E.M. Woodward.
    › John Black's Cedar Swamp: Located in the middle of Obhannon (also called Bear Swamp). Its bridge was below J.B. Cedar Swamp. J.B. Cedar Swamp was listed on a Monmouth County deed in 1749, defined as a point on the south side of Cedar Swamp. It was then called Bear Swamp or Obhannon and is the beginning of Black Cedar Swamp. This tract was conveyed to Patterson Lumber Company Inc. before it became part of a state wildlife management area.
    › Thomas and John Black owned a gristmill in Manalapan Township circa 1823, according to the book *History of Monmouth County* by Franklin Ellis (1885). (Black's Mill's post village was named for John Black, most likely a different Black than the Black who owned the cedar swamp.)
- Joseph Woolston Brick (1804–February 1, 1847): A clerk at Batsto from 1826 to 1830. His daughter Josephine E.

Brick, born on July 4, 1844, operated Bergen Iron Works in
Lakewood, New Jersey, from 1833 to 1865.

- John Bray: From New Brunswick. In 1802, he bought part
  of Three Partners Mill in the area known as Lakewood
  in the Pines. The town had a number of names over
  the centuries; Three Partners Mill, Bergen Iron Works,
  Bricksburg and Lakewood.
- Joseph Bonaparte (January 7, 1768–July 28, 1844): He lived in
  America from 1817 to 1832 and was involved in land speculation.
- John B. Beach, around 1872, owned land in the Jackson and
  Lakewood area, as reported by author Paul Axel-Lute, who
  wrote the 1986 book *Lakewood-In-The-Pines*.

Down we went, one rabbit hole after another. There was one name we
didn't add to the list, even though it had been an early guess around the
kitchen round table. That name was John, or Lord Berkeley. He, being
the ruling power over West Jersey before there was a unified New Jersey,
lost that title in 1702. An imaginary line called the Keith line of 1686 was
drawn farther to the west than the Lawrence line of 1743 (which, on a map,
goes directly through the area of Hessian Island and the J.B. marker). Both
surveyed lines would have had markers to distinguish the property, much
like property stones today. Was the J.B. marker part of one of the surveyed
lines that created an East and a West Jersey? Does J.B. refer to Lord John
Berkeley? That's too absurd of a guess. Or is it?

Or maybe if you have a wild imagination, it's a gravestone marker, and
the initials J.B. refer to Captain John Bacon, an infamous Pine Robber
who may have worked the same stagecoach route that passed by the area
of Hessian Island. This was one of the many hideouts the Tory refugees
secretly operated out of. Local tradition in Plumsted Township names
Success Road "Stagecoach Road"; it meanders through the neighborhood
and cuts through the same land that the Pine Robbers would have had to
travel to get to Borden's Run and the site we discovered. But who would
haul a piece of ironstone that size across a hard-to-navigate swamp and
cranberry bog to carve the initials J.B. in it and dedicate it to a person who
would steal from both friend and foe? A more plausible guess surfaced in the
stack of papers and names revealed on a map that read "Borden's Run." An
older map revealed the area was officially labeled "Borden's Mill Branch,"
which is the waterway that eventually leads out to Barnegat Bay via the Toms
River. There in Vivian Zinkin's book *Place Names of Ocean County New Jersey*

Dirt roads once led travelers along stagecoach routes. *Author's collection.*

1609–1849, the author writes, "Borden's Mill Branch 1867 named for John Borden, mill owner. Since the Borden family–owned property, including a gristmill, was in this area before 1768, the stream probably bore the name Borden from that time." Could it be that the J.B. ironstone marker is just a plain old—albeit very old—land marker?

That sounds very logical and reasonable, but there's a twist. In one of the stacks of historical documents, there is a mention of one king of Spain with the initials J.B., who resided in Bordentown, New Jersey. He was into land acquisition and speculation while he lived in his adopted city. Bordentown just so happens to be where the kin of John Borden, a man named Joseph Borden, resided. Could it be that a Borden descendant transferred a deed to the famous Joseph Bonaparte, who had a newly (it was new back then but is ancient today) installed ironstone land marker with his initials on it? It is quite possible, but the connection to Joseph Bonaparte and the Borden family isn't there unless you force the idea, for Joseph Borden was long dead before Bonaparte came to Bordentown, New Jersey. Several other land speculators and investors with the initials J.B. appear in historical books, such as Salter's *History of Monmouth and Ocean Counties, New Jersey*, but the connections of these individuals would be pure speculation, not even educated guesses. On a deed search at first the Ocean County Clerk's Office, which goes back to only 1850 (thanks Mrs. Ruth Shertenlieb) and then on to the Monmouth County Clerk's Office (Ocean County wasn't founded until 1850), a deed in the vicinity of our J.B. marker reads like Egyptian hieroglyphics, but the name attached is plain as day: John Black's Cedar Swamp, 1749.

While this may not be as romantic or exciting as J.B. referring to a lord and proprietor of West Jersey or the brother of Napoleon Bonaparte, the red ironstone marker in a cedar brake out in the middle of nowhere (but what once was somewhere) is probably just a property marker. The private landowner was probably one of the last to own the parcel of land before the State of New Jersey collected dozens of private owners' land deeds, just like it in the vicinity, and combined them to make Colliers Mills Wildlife Management Area in Jackson, New Jersey. So, it is either a leftover property marker for Mr. John Black from 1749 or a subsequent owner John Borden from 1867. Both had the crisp, cool waters of Borden's Run flowing across today's open cranberry bogs and an enclosed white cedar swamp, both natural resources harvested for bygone industries.

Rabbit hunting, we will go, till finally, we suppose, we have eliminated all possible answers and find the right rabbit. Even though we dug through historical documents and reviewed maps and deeds at multiple county clerk's offices, we got only a glimpse of the mystery of the J.B. ironstone marker and saw nothing of the local legend of the place called Hessian Island. Months later, we made a monumental discovery in an out-of-print book from 1863 titled *History of Burlington and Mercer Counties, New Jersey, with Biographical Sketches by Major E.M. Woodward and John F. Hageman*. It was there that we found our hare. And it was wild to find—like a sliver of hair in a salad the waiter just brought out of the kitchen. If we didn't get that wild hair up our you-know-what, who knows where this story would have languished? Possibly on the writer's desk, unfinished and unread. Wild hair—well, I really mean wild hare.

Back to that legend of the Hessian Island hideaway in the Pines and forgotten treasures. The J.B. marker was a mere distraction from the mystery of Pine Robbers and buried treasures. America's struggles for its independence are well documented. War, broadly speaking, cares little about borders and the land families inhabit. One family can be on either side of a border, looking directly at each other, but seeing two different views. In America, neighbors and family members were pitted against each other, especially in New Jersey, where George Washington and the Continental army spent a good amount of time fighting the British army. Tories were colonists who saw the Crown as the highest power, and Whigs were colonists who saw the Declaration of Independence as the word of the land. The rise of a tit-for-tat attitude, or, in more historical terminology, privateering, was occurring on both sides of the war. Many a Whig and countryman who favored independence from the Crown took to either sponsoring or captaining a ship in the enterprise of privateering. Privateering was a close sister to pirating. And both were stepsisters to Pine Robbers, who rode on horseback through the Pine Barrens in lieu of traversing the open seas on a ship.

The book *History of Burlington and Mercer Counties, New Jersey, with Biographical Sketches by Major E.M. Woodward and John F. Hageman* states:

> *A party of armed Tories, or "Pine Robbers," on the 15th of August, 1780, says the* New Jersey Gazette, *"came to the house of John Black Jr., in Springfield, Burlington County, and robbed him of a considerable sum of hard money, also sundry wearing apparel. From Mr. Black's they proceeded to the house of Caleb Shreve, Esq., taking with them a certain Mr. Llyod as a guide, or to prevent his giving information to the neighborhood. They robbed Mr. Shreve of a small sum of hard and Continental money, but did not take anything else. From Mr. Shreve's they went to the house of Mr. Cleayton Newbold, whom they robbed of a small quantity of plate, a gold watch, and money. From Mr. Cleayton Newbold's they passed to the house of Mr. William Newbold, when observing a number of people about the house, they feigned themselves to be Whigs and in quest of horse-thieves, and did not attempt to rob." Col. William Shreve, of the First Regiment, Burlington State Troops, who resided near Recklesstown, aroused the inhabitants and pursued them to the Pines, where, at Borden's Run, they were brought to skirmish, wounding two and capturing one, besides several firelocks and most of the plunder.*

Was this the proverbial smoking gun to a local legend? The needle in a haystack was found. Is this evidence that Hessian Island was the hideout of one of the gangs that marauded across South Jersey and hid in the dense swampland of the Pines in colonial days? This one entry about the skirmish at Borden's Run is the only lifeline found in researching this story for over three years. Today, the road to Hessian Island is overgrown, and the walk of several miles through bogs and cedar groves is picturesque; it's a Robin Hood–like hideout in the forest. Was this home to John Bacon, one of those who was known to terrorize the countryside in the name of a British monarch? Note the remarks from authors Edwin Salter and George C. Beekman in an 1887 book *Old Times in Old Monmouth: Historical Reminiscences of Old Monmouth County, New Jersey*:

> *In ancient papers we have found notices of refugee raids in Burlington county, but they do not give the names of the leaders. It is probable that Bacon commanded some of these expeditions as he was well acquainted in Burlington, and his wife resided at Pemberton in the latter part of the war. About September 1782, it is announced that a man, supposed to be a spy of Bacon's, was shot in the woods near Pemberton, by some of the inhabitants who went out to hunt him; and we find that the citizens of Burlington were so much exasperated against him that they organized expeditions to follow him in old Monmouth.*

The present treasures on display are rare old cedar trees and wild orchids that grow here and there along this once road to somewhere; today, it seems to be a road to nowhere. But what else could be hidden in the dense evergreen jungle, where Pine Robbers once sat around a fire, splitting up shiny gold and silver plates? And does the story of the ironstone J.B. marker end there, too?

The following documented revolutionary-period skirmish took place in 1780. A quick trip to the New Jersey State Library revealed the *Collins New Jersey Gazette* on microfiche dated August 23, 1780; this is the original source of the aforementioned quote in the 1883 book *History of Burlington and Mercer Counties, New Jersey, with Biographical Sketches*. Scanning the microfiche revealed a few more details but not many. And scanning through 1780, 1781 and 1782 printings from the *New Jersey Gazette* reveals no follow-up to the original print story detailing the robbery in Springfield that ended at Borden's Run in Monmouth County. The robbery occurred on the evening of Thursday, August 17, 1780. This author also contacted the Library of Congress, which shared notes about the publication but also could not find any follow-up to the story in *Collins Gazette*: "As a general note, this newspaper began production in Burlington, New Jersey, but was moved to Trenton, New Jersey, in March

An Atlantic white cedar swamp. *Author's collection.*

1778. From our records and what I can see digitized in the database, this was a weekly paper published on Wednesdays."

A few interesting details from the original source paper reveal that after making a quick getaway, the Pine Robbers were chased.

> *Col. William Shreve, with a number of the inhabitants, immediately set off in pursuit of the villains, and overtook them at Borden's Run on the verge of the pines, in a thick swamp. Mr. John De Cow observing their sentinel, hail'd him, who answered by the discharge of his musket, and ran into the swamp; Mr. De Cow returned the fire, and pursued him to closely that he threw away his gun and plunder, among which was all Mr. Newbold's plate and Mr. Black's continental money and apparel. One of the robbers it is said is since taken and lodged in the Monmouth gaol.*

The names of the four armed men who came to the house of John Black Jr. in Springfield, Burlington County, that Thursday evening in 1780 escape us today. They were smart enough to feign themselves Whigs in pursuit of horse thieves when confronted with too large of an opposition at the residence of William Newbold. They then outran Colonel Shreve and reached their pine hideout, narrowly escaping capture in a shootout.

All but one as reported in the *New Jersey Gazette*. But still, time has guarded their identities and what their real motives were, besides theft. American Revolution historians will tell you that finding documents to corroborate a historical footnote is difficult at best and, sometimes, near impossible. Searching the Monmouth County Archives for a jail (or gaol) record of the sole Pine Robber who was reportedly turned over to the Monmouth gaol is like trying to find a needle in a haystack.

If you know your American Revolutionary history, especially the key parts New Jersey played, you'll remember that prior to this incident, in 1780, there were many battles fought, some won and some lost by the rebels, or Patriots. There was the 1776 Battle of Trenton in December, which brilliantly gave breath to a struggling campaign led by George Washington. And there were other battles won by the ragamuffins of ole George, like the 1777 Battle of Princeton and yet another win for the independence of the colonies the following year at the Battle of Monmouth. Loyalists and regular British soldiers alike were in no mood to continue their loses; thus, each personally felt humiliated and wanted to strike out in revenge. After all, retaliation was the law of the land on both sides. The Continental Congress, in April 1778, passed laws that said it was legal to seize the lands and homes of known fugitives and offenders and subsequently sell off those properties. This only invigorated the Loyalists' angst against their once friends and neighbors.

The British retaliated against the privateers, supporting the abandonment of British rule at the Battle of Chestnut Neck in 1778. Hundreds of people were involved in pirating in the waters between New York and New Jersey, utilizing the Mullica River Basin all throughout the American Revolution. The small village of Chestnut Neck served as a distribution point for the commandeered bounty from the open sea. Much like the Pine Robbers were doing by way of piccarooning throughout the colony concentrated in Burlington and Monmouth Counties near the safety of the New Jersey Pine Barrens. Privateering basically legalized being a pirate, a person who sailed on the open seas and along the rivers of New Jersey. John Bacon and other Tory refugee Pine Robbers were inland, working the land supply chain of goods that were going to be auctioned at places like Freehold, Mount Holly and Allentown, New Jersey. John, besides being ruthless, was also cunning and had many characteristics of a military leader. He was known as the "Tory Outlaw," Captain John Bacon, but eventually, he rose to such prominence that in the early 1780s, New Jersey governor William Livingston called him public enemy no. 1 and offered a bounty for his capture and that of many other Tory refuges. In April 1780, it was reported that John Bacon and his gang had robbed the house of John Holmes in upper Freehold and, afterward, went south to Manahawkin, attacking and killing several Patriots there. Another well-documented account of John Bacon from the fall of 1780 charges him with the death of Captain Joshua Studson. Salter's book *History of Monmouth and Ocean Counties, New Jersey* said of Bacon,

> *Himself, and men were well acquainted with the roads and paths through the forests of Burlington and old Monmouth, and had numerous hiding places, cabins, caves, &c., in the woods and swamps, where they could remain until some trustworthy spy informed them of a safe chance to venture out on what was then termed a picarooning expedition.*

We don't have the names of the banditti from this incident, but we do know the location of their capture: their hideout. It's not a far stretch to say that the infamous John Bacon could have been one of the banditti whom Colonel William Shreve (1737–1813) caught up with at Hessian Island in August 1780. The sentinel's musket blast alerted the rest of the Pine Robbers of the imminent danger of being caught, so they abandoned the camp that we suppose is the Hessian Island of local lore. And we know the men who were robbed at gunpoint: John Black Jr., Caleb Shreve, Mr. Lloyd and Mr. Cleayton Newbold. What do we know about the victims? Why did the unnamed Pine Robbers choose Springfield, New Jersey, and how did they pick the area known as Hessian Island for their hideout in the Pines? And can we place one of the well-known Pine Robbers, like John Bacon, at the site? Was he possibly the leader of this foray into Springfield, crossing over from one county to the next?

Generally, it's known that Tory refugees targeted those on the opposing team (i.e., the Patriots). In the Springfield area, Shreve family members held high-profile leadership positions in George Washington's army. Colonel Wm. Shreve, who gave chase, had suffered a total loss of his property (it was all plundered and burned) in Burlington County, just prior, on June 23, 1778, at the hands of the British army. The two Newbold men who were targeted were also prominent men: Cleayton Newbold was a member of the Council of Proprietors of West Jersey. This alone could have been incentive enough for the likes of John Bacon or another Tory sympathizer to wanted to rob these families in Springfield in August 1780. John Bacon died by hanging in Burlington County in 1783. The county residents had an extreme prejudice against this man. One account says that when John Bacon was finally caught and hanged, they wanted to bury him under the crossroads on Arney's Mount in Springfield Township; that way, they thought, he would never have peace in the afterlife. Another account says that John Bacon's body was given to his brother to be buried in an unknown location. This would have been done out of respect for the brother, who was in good standing in the community. Circumstantial evidence has the reader jumping to the conclusion that it was John Bacon who led this gang of Pine Robbers and stole away to Hessian Island.

And what about the location of Hessian Island that has the Lawrence line cutting through it? Is that a random part of the countryside or an expertly designed site for a hideaway of Pine Robbers? There's a claim that the J.B. marker is a property marker for a John Black, the owner of Black's Cedar Swamp. Or it could be a headstone for Captain John Bacon, a notorious outlaw. But wait, wasn't there another Black descendant involved in the story? It was a John Black Jr. who was reportedly robbed by the Pine Robbers in Springfield, Burlington County. This robbery eventually led to a shootout at the Borden's Run area, or Hessian Island, in Monmouth County (Ocean County today). It would have added insult to injury to rob one Black in Burlington County and then retreat to another Black's property in old Monmouth County. The *New Jersey Gazette* reported that both Newbold

The scene of a Pine Robber hideout—if you believe in the fables of old. *Author's collection.*

and John Black Jr.'s property was returned. It makes you think that it's an awful coincidence the Pine Robbers hid out at a property owned by John Black. Speaking of the knowledge of where the Lawrence line went through southern New Jersey, would it be too far-fetched to say that Mr. Cleayton Newbold, a member of the Council of Proprietors, would have known the area that the banditti who robbed Springfield residents, including himself, Mr. John Black Jr. and others, escaped to? And would John Black Jr. have known the area if he knew the John Black of John Black Cedar Swamp, the deed owner of what is now the Colliers Mills Wildlife Management Area? That is a mystery in itself.

Tale of Three Men Named John Lawrence

There's another point of interest to the location where Colonel Shreve and the posse from Springfield finally overtook the Pine Robbers. That location within the vicinity (today's technology says five thousand feet) of the 1743 surveyed Lawrence line may have lent its remoteness to people of nefarious wants who needed to hide from the public. Ellis wrote:

> *They had their hiding-places and headquarters in caves burrowed in the sand; along the borders of swamps, and in other spots so secluded and masked by nature as to be comparatively safe from detection; and from these places they went forth, usually by night, in bands and individually, to rob, burn and murder; so that, for defense against these worse than Indian prowlers, the people of the county were obliged to keep their firearms constantly by them at their work in the fields, at their meetings for worship, and by their bedsides at night.*

The man connected to the last survey line also spent time in the Burlington County Jail for being a Tory sympathizer—and worse. Were the hideouts in the Pines that stretched across several counties and safeguarded the Tory refugees not randomly selected by outlaw leaders like John Bacon but assisted by someone who knew the land, had two sons enlisted in the British army and wanted to assist King George III in squashing the rebellion, once and for all? John Lawrence (1709–1794) was such a man. Franklin Ellis's book *History of Monmouth County, New Jersey*, states:

Being advanced in years at the beginning of the Revolution, Mr. Lawrence did not bear arms, but he accepted from the British the important service of issuing Royalist protections to such Americans as he was able to induce to adjure the cause of their country and swear allegiance to Great Britain, for which he was arrested by the committee, and confined for nine months in Burlington jail. He died in 1794, at the age of eighty-five years.

Certainly, surveyor John Lawrence would have known the land along the Lawrence line like no other. The book *Ocean County Four Centuries in the Making*, by Pauline Miller (2000), reports:

John Lawrence rode horseback through the pines carrying a brass surveying instrument in a wooden box in his saddle bag. The compass had to be removed from the box, joined together and set up for him to sight his line while chain bearers chopped down brush and small trees to give him a clear path for his site line. These barriers measured the line with an iron link and chain sixty-six feet long which they dragged through the rough pine forest floor over rocks for the entire distance across New Jersey from Long Beach Island to just south of the Delaware Water Gap.

John Lawrence, the surveyor general in 1743, ran the last line across New Jersey that was ultimately adopted over the 1686 Keith line recorded by Surveyor General George Keith for deed purposes, even though New Jersey had been unified by the early 1700s. Before he was officially charged and jailed, Mr. John Lawrence was subject to a house arrest of sorts by the Provincial Congress, or the Convention of New Jersey, on July 5, 1776: "Ordered, That the President do take the parole of honour of Mr. John Lawrence, of Monmouth County, not to depart the house of Mr. Renssellier Williams; and, if Mr. Lawrence should refuse to give the same, that the President order him to be confirmed under such guard as he may deem necessary."

The second John Brown Lawrence Esq. (1729–1796) of Burlington, New Jersey, was a lawyer and member of the Provincial Council of New Jersey (1771–75). As the mayor of Burlington before the Revolutionary War (in 1769), he was a Loyalist who spent his time, like his uncle John Lawrence, in the Burlington County Jail for his part in the American Revolution. Mayor Lawrence's uncle John Lawrence was also living the parallel life of a Tory refugee supporter and Loyalist sympathizer in Old Monmouth. John B. Larence later moved to Canada. Author Pierce's book *Smugglers' Woods* says this about Mayor John B. Lawrence:

> [A]*n ardent Tory, who later ceremoniously welcomed British and Hessian officers but whose door was closed to patriot legislators. The Rev. Jonathan Odell, Tory rector of St. Mary's Church, who was to play a shabby role in the Benedict Arnold treason plot, was politically and socially active in ostracizing the unwelcome legislators. Another prominent Burlington Tory was Daniel Coxe, who later led in organizing loyalist harassment of his former neighbors and friends.*

This third John Lawrence was the son of surveyor John Lawrence. In this instance, the phrase "like father like son" rings true. Dr. John Lawrence (1747–1830) was a noted Loyalist. Ellis's *History of Monmouth County* states, "In 1776 he was arrested by order of General Washington and was ordered by the Provincial Congress of New Jersey to remain at Trenton on parole, but he was afterwards permitted to remove to Morristown." The youngest son of John Lawrence the surveyor was Elisha Lawrence, born 1740. He had the same Loyalist views and was credited with recruiting five hundred men to the British side. He also served as a colonel of the First Battalion in the New Jersey Royal Volunteers. The Lawrence family line of division stretched far and wide, supporting the status quo of the country being a group of British colonies.

THE FACTS AS THEY are outlined in this story are clear. There was a robbery carried out by four persons on Thursday, August 17, 1780, in the northwest section of Springfield, Burlington County, during the American Revolution, as reported in the *New Jersey Gazette*. Patriot Colonel Shreve of Burlington County chased and caught up with said robbers, and a skirmish occurred at Borden's Run, which today is part of Ocean County and within the borders of Colliers Mills Wildlife Management Area in Jackson, New Jersey. Local tradition, which is murky on facts at best and substantiated by oral history, suggests the area of the skirmish is known as Hessian Island, which is also in an area that intersects the Lawrence line of 1743. Would individual members of the Council of Proprietors of West Jersey have known where the Lawrence line began in a bordering county? Can we assume the Pine Robbers in the American Revolution were more organized than we thought? It was a known tactic to punish the dwellings of colonists who took up arms against the king. Would a Tory sympathizer named John Lawrence give intelligence to leaders against the colonial rebellion during the American Revolution? This information would have enabled them to utilize strategic base camps in remote sections of southern New Jersey. And the three John Lawrences and other noted Loyalists drew another lesser-known line that divided the state between East and West Jersey. In a most sinister way, it was a divisional line in the budding nation, pitting friend against friend and countryman against countryman.

Was the Tory refugee and Pine Robber hideout of Hessian Island evidence of a coordinated effort by the Lawrence family, who, before the war, didn't believe in the taxation the mother country was heaping on the colonies, like their fellow colonists? Yet they became staunch Loyalists in the end, coming down on the wrong side of history by passively aiding the targeting of militiamen and Patriots' homes in the hopes of defeating them from within. This caused local turmoil, drawing the attention of soldiers home instead of allowing them to focus on the mission to support George Washington and the country's rebellion. And out of all the possible names the initials J.B. could stand for on the marker in a cedar swamp near the Lawrence line known locally as Hessian Island, could they refer to none other than Captain John Bacon, one of the most famous Tory refugee leaders? This lends credence to the theory that it was a more coordinated effort, supporting the mission of the Pine Robbers in a way that has not been suggested in previous historical literature. These are questions we may never know the full answers to. Much of what is suggested is pure speculation on the part of this author—some would say it's a flight of fancy. One of the most frustrating and, at the same time, fun things about local history is that there are always more details to uncover, more rabbit holes to wander down. The end of the story is just the beginning.

26

DON'T LET OLD SNAG GET YOU!

A titan of the dried floral industry in New Jersey, John Richardson, employed hundreds of Piney families in southern New Jersey, harvesting 101 pineycraft plants for the industry. He would tell you to just call him Jack. He had an interesting hobby, one that is near extinct today. If you asked Jack what's the best tool for hunting raccoons, he'd say, "You gotta have a good coon dog from down south." Back in the late '70s and early '80s, raccoon hunting was akin to fox hunting on the level of grandeur. Sportsmen from all over came to the Pines to coon hunt. Fox hunting was prevalent in the Pines, too, but that didn't appeal to Jack and his friends. You see, these fellas had interesting hobbies, like playing poker and staying out late. Well, coon hunting is a night owl hobby, too, and Jack always spent a considerable amount of money on purchasing the best tool for the job. In the case of coon hunting, this is a bluetick coonhound.

Even if he didn't have a lot of money at the time, Jack had to have the best dogs. Straight out of Virginia, these hunting dogs were known for their prowess in treeing a raccoon once they got the scent of one. Coon hunters hunt with coonhounds, and fox hunters hunt with foxhounds. Hunting for foxes and raccoons has all but become a thing of the past. Today, a neighbor would call the police if they saw men with flashlights traversing a field at 3:00 a.m.

One story that many a friend of Jack Richardson have heard him tell over and over involves an adventure with his competitor, harness horse racing driver and good friend Ed Kelley. The two men went out late one night to hunt raccoons in New Egypt, New Jersey, which had a lot of open space and

Raccoon of Snag Legend.
Artist, Shane Tomalinas.

farmland. There was an area at the edge of the southwest portion of the town, off Brindletown Road, that local hunters called Old Snag. Old Snag earned its name because of its twenty-foot-high wall of cat briers followed by a Pine Barrens swamp that was all but impossible to travel through on foot. Gustav Kobbe's 1889 book *The New Jersey Coast and Pines* has a map with a pinpoint in this area labeled "Head of Snag." John might have been fond of the area, as he was born not too far from there at Brindle Park near Brindle Lake.

A hunting buddy and anonymous South Jersey farmer retold one of Jack's favorite hunting tales:

> *There was a dog named Rock from Virginia who chased a coon right into Old Snag, and Jack and Ed lost the dog. Next thing you know, it's 3:00 a.m. and fog rolled in, and old Rock was still treeing a coon, but they*

An Old Snag briar tangle. *Author's collection.*

A masked bandit.
Author's collection.

couldn't get to the dog. Both guys get stuck in Old Snag and barely get out at 6:30 a.m. the next morning. So, they left Jack's coat there for the coon dog to come back. [A good coon dog is trained to return to the scent of its owner when it gets separated.] *Jack and Ed come back the following day* [to Old Snag] *around 4:30 p.m., and sure enough they could still hear the coon dog treeing something. Several days after, on the fifth day, it was still treeing the raccoon, but they couldn't get to the dog. On the sixth day, there was silence—Jack had paid $3,100 for that dog, and they had lost poor old Rock.*

Now, like any good fishing tale, hunting tales have a small measure of exaggeration, but here's how Jack told the story. Some five years later, the same thing happened again. They had a dog named Candy run across the same field into Old Snag. It seemed to be the same area, possibly the same tree. This time, the pair of hunters went in another way to find the dog. They shone the flashlight up in the tree and shot a coon that Candy had treed. Then they looked over to the tree next and saw it had a skeleton of a dog with a collar at its base. They shined the light up to the top of the tree and saw a coon skeleton. "Son of a gun—if that wasn't ole Rock, who died treeing that raccoon that also succumbed to lack of water and starved in the tree, not being able to get away from the coonhound."

It was a tragic ending that represented the value put on a good hunting dog.[13]

27

OLD MAN BUCKY ROMAN'S GHOST

America's transportation systems and the birth of new technologies and evolutions of travel have enabled the country to grow and create wealth unimaginable in other countries. Our infrastructure is as important to our everyday livelihoods as this nation's marvelous inventions and the men and women who invented them. Without the ability to move things from one place to another by the cheapest means available, growth would come to a halt. To spur growth, not too long ago, we leaned on the railroad system. Those iron tracks literally had spurs, officially called rail spurs, and could handle the popular main line used for public transit, with its cabin cars and another track that led to the front doors of budding industries. The railroad served all in the community and met each new demand head-on. But today, the railroad of old has seen better days and most of its glory years are far behind us.

The ghostly abandoned rails now attract wanderers who seek things to do off the beaten path. Those who love to discover and explore an abandoned site don't have to look too far for an old railroad station—they just need to trace the miles and miles of abandoned tracks dotting the landscape. This is true of New Jersey and most states across the country. It's too expensive to remove the heavy, unpainted steel rails and the wooden ties beneath the tons of rusty, red track. They lay where they are hoping to one day rise again and begin life anew. This is wishful thinking, perhaps. If you're a believer in paranormal activity, a trip to the local abandoned track brings excitement and fresh food for the overactive imagination to eat. Sometimes, things that

Tracks of Yesterday. *Artist, Shane Tomalinas.*

are supposed to be dead don't stay that way. Like they say, things aren't always as they seem. The following story involves the abandoned Central New Jersey Southern Railroad that once ran the distance from Red Bank, New Jersey, to Delaware Bay.

Near where our story takes place, the Whiting Junction Station once stood. Not only did the Central Southern Division roll on by, but other rails, like the Pennsylvania Railroad and the Tuckerton Railroad, could be connected to other lines travelling in different directions. Hundreds of thousands of people from the big cities of Philadelphia and New York rode these rails simultaneously. But now, ghosts' feet balance on the single steel track. Maybe slightly more importantly, those rails moved commerce. Locally, one of the staple businesses was one you'd never guess: Allyn's Manufacturing of Whiting, New Jersey. It was a pinecone factory of sorts, located just around the corner from Whiting Junction Station, which sat on one of the only highways that intersected and cut through the Pines, north to south, along

Railroad tracks in the Pines. *Author's collection.*

Route 539. Pineballs, or pinecones as they're more commonly called, were a big business in the Whiting area. Whiting was at the gateway of the New Jersey Pine Barrens and was perfectly situated just fifteen miles north of Warren Grove, the home of over twenty square miles of pygmy pine forest. There was a hustling industry of dried flowers and plant material, harvested by local people. There were over thirteen thousand acres of chest-high pitch pine trees that held hundreds of thousands of closed brown pinecones. It was an unlimited supply for the dried flora industry.

The owners of Allyn's Manufacturing were two gentlemen from Brooklyn, New York: Allen Golin and Louis Landwehr. Being greenhorns, they weren't used to dealing with locals known as Pineys, who drove beat-up cars and trucks with bumper stickers on them that read "Proud to be a Piney from My Nose to My Hiney." But they knew an industry was budding, and there was money to be had. They bought their first load of pinecones from one of those Pineys, a man named Royden Roosevelt Romans (1904–1966). He was known as Old Man Bucky Romans by other Pineys, but to Allen and Louis, he was Roy Romans, an answer to their language barrier with the locals. So, they hired someone who was one of the Pineys and became their number-one buyer. Romans was born a Philadelphian but died a Jerseyman. He was born in Philadelphia, Pennsylvania, on February 3, 1904; there, he, with his mother, Ida, and father, Thomas Romans, stayed for a year and half, then moved to Pasadena Village, New Jersey. He also had an older brother named Clarence. He grew up relatively poor; his parents never owned a home and reportedly always rented. But through perseverance and hard work, Royden Romans owned his own home in 1940, seven years after he lost both of his parents in Manchester, New Jersey, with only a fourth-grade education. He could read and write and was an accomplished man by all standards.

In the *Newark Sunday News*, on December 17, 1961, famed New Jersey historian, author and reporter John Cunningham wrote an article titled "Pine Cones by the Millions: Jersey's Gift to Holidays." He wrote about his interview with Royden Romans. "Pineballing can be done to some extent the year around," Mr. Romans declared. "But most do it September to April. You don't go pineballing when you can go a hunting sphagnum moss in the spring. You don't go when you can be huckleberrying or cranberrying. You go after the frost kills the cranberries and there's nothing else to do." He was a man who knew the woods as well as any other and better than most, for he was buying pinecones and selling them before Allyn Manufacturing Company even existed. In his once-three-acre yard that is now divided by Good Luck Road in Whiting, New Jersey, the pinecones he picked or bought

As a change from 7,000,000 pine cones, Allen Galin and Louis Landwehr admire silver-coated ruscus, another of the many decorative products of their plant at Whitings.

Royden Romans, veteran boss of the "pineballing" operation, demonstrates use of heavy gloves and metal tub to withstand wear and tear of tough pine cone stickers.

Oscar Payne shovels "popped" cones into baskets for bagging and shipment. RIGHT: Pine cones are tightly closed at time of picking but open after five hours in oven at 200 degrees.

Top: Images from the December 17, 1961 article "Pine Cones by the Millions: Jersey's Gift To Holidays," written by John Cunningham. *Copyright* Newark News.

Bottom: Once the logo of Allyn's Manufacturing, Whiting, New Jersey. *Author's collection.*

from other Pineys were spread out on the ground, where the sun would eventually open them. It was said he sold the opened cones to florists and collected the seeds and sold them to the state parks before he was hired by Allen Golin and Louis Landwehr of Allyn's Manufacturing Company. Several years later, after Mr. Romans had died and his nephew had sold his home to a new owner, John Hurley, strange occurrences were reported on the property. The following story was relayed to Romans's niece Lois by her uncle John, who recently passed in 2021. It raises the hairs on the back of one's neck. Lois retells the story here for the first time.

The strangest things happened while we were building our house on the property. The original two-story home was forest green, and it really blended in with the pine and oak forest around it. And there was a garage that only had black tar paper for siding. We lived in the original home for a short period before our home was built and then we tore down the old home. The only original part of the property was the tar paper garage we kept. The garage was situated to the south end of the house which is where there was also not too far behind it an abandoned railroad spur. I would be in the garage and my tools would go missing or be moved from one place on the wall where I last left it and come to find it on the other side of the room hanging on the wall. It really freaked me out. But the worst was when, suddenly, late in the evening, I'd be out in the garage, and back yonder, where the railroad tracks were, I heard horses like a stagecoach passing by. I stopped using the garage for a while because of it.

Then—you're not going to believe me when I tell you this—but one day, a young woman shows up. I'll never forget it; she's dressed in a floral print sundress, and it's a beautiful afternoon. I just finished lunch outside. She comes strolling around the garage to stand on the patio in front of me. She greets me and gives her name: Ms. Daisy Webb. She handed me an old newspaper clipping, and in it, there's a two-page article about the previous owner, Mr. Royden Romans. We're talking casually enough, and she seems to be normal to me, so no alarms are going off. But when she starts to describe Royden, it's as if she knew the guy personally. She said, "Romans was about your height, five feet, ten inches, built like the pitch pines around here. When the wind blowed, his limbs bent like the pine boughs, for he was a spindle of a man. But he had piercing brown eyes that reminded you of the puppy in the window, the one you felt bad for and had to take home with you. And there was that tiny scar on his cheek from pulling a pinecone on a branch that didn't want to let go, so he get got wacked in the face." Uncle John, feeling at ease speaking to the woman, mentions out loud as he's staring at

Pitch pine trees in Warren Grove, New Jersey. *Author's collection.*

the black tarpapered garage, "Mmm…the hauntings might be the previous owner then."

Without skipping a beat, the young woman continued, "I bet you didn't know, because I didn't tell you, that Roy was smart as a whip. He really was a good boy and a good man. Do you know, at four years old, he made the Giberson Mill School honor roll, but later, because he had to help support his parents, he left school in the fourth grade. If he's haunting this place, there's got to be a good reason."

Uncle John asked Daisy, "Why don't he go haunt that god forsaken desert the Pineys call the Evergreen Sea—down the Plains?"

She replied, "I traveled all this way to help you find out. Can we look in the garage I walked by earlier?" Uncle John got up from the table, and the two of them walked over to the garage, and she said, "The new house you built is beautiful. It would be too fancy for Roy, but I like it. That was one thing about Roy—he was too plain for many people's tastes around here, if you know what I mean." Uncle John didn't know what she meant by that, but before he could ask, his uninvited guest blurted out, "There, up there in the corner, do you see that tub?"

Well sure enough, to the surprise of Uncle John there was a bucket or a tub hanging in the way back corner. He'd been in and out of that garage a hundred times and never seen it. There wasn't any window in that section of the garage, so it was dark and cold. "Let me get the stepladder to take it down."

When he brought it down, he grunted from the weight and tried to balance himself without falling as he stepped down. Then they both walked out of the garage with it into the warm sunlight. Now in the light, you could see it was a round galvanized tub, probably an antique now. And on one side of the old metal tub, there were a pair of heavy-duty gray gloves draped over the top rim. Looking inside the tub, it was loaded near to the top with a mess of gray pinecones. Uncle John spoke first, "Well, I'll be. I never noticed that tub before. And look at all those pinecones. Why you suppose they're not opened by now?"

Ms. Daisy replied, "Ole Roy could tell you, and I think that's what he's been trying to do by moving your tools around from one wall to another as you said. I know a little about Piney work, and those pinecones need fire to open or be out in the sun to bake in high summer heat for the glue that binds them to loosen and let their seed fall to the ground to grow another generation. Roy watched that one thousand times over—one of his favorite things to do I guess here on Good Luck Road, which really wasn't much luck to poor Roy. I suppose this was his last pineballing tub before he killed himself right there in that black tarpapered garage."

Uncle John exclaimed, "Royden killed himself in there? How come? And how do I get him to quit haunting the place."

Ms. Daisy considered the man's questions, then answered, "Roy was said to have a crush on a woman who had grander tastes then him. Jilted is the word his last employer used. Roy to me was a beautiful man, but the life he built along those old railroad tracks wasn't everyone's cup of tea. If I knew Roy, he must have forgotten about those cones, and it's been at him ever since. Best if you toss them on an open fire and let them burn. God knows if Roy's feeling the same fire for taking his own life." Uncle John whispered, "Poor soul." Ms. Daisy, nodding in agreement, said to Uncle John, "The tracks to the back of your garage are yours now but Roy's before. Railroad steel and crossties are gone, and all you can make out is the outline of the railroad bed, but that don't mean the way ahead doesn't continue. Many lost souls walk all day and all night, balancing on that single steel track, as if they're riding the evening train back home or going on vacation down the Jersey Shore. Oh, so simpler times. Rust and all don't matter to the pitter-patter of our feet. If you can, it'd be best if you got that fire a started and let those pinecones be blessed with a kiss by fire furling the seeds of tomorrow and settling poor boy Roy's spirit free."

Opened pinecones. *Author's collection.*

Uncle John looked at the odd duck who stood in his backyard, asking him to burn ancient pinecones in the fire pit, but he didn't disobey. The rest of the story, as Uncle John tells it, is as he reached for the lighter from the patio deck, where he left his lunch, the woman must have ran away, for as he turned with lighter in hand, she was gone. He lit that fire and dumped a handful of closed pinecones in the hot fire and took a seat while watching the cones open with a crackle and a pop. Each time a cone opened, a blast of pine seeds took wing. He had lost track of time, and evening was now fast approaching. What a strange day he had experienced with the woman named Ms. Daisy Webb. The blaze grew bright, with the resin from the pinecones washing everything around it in a soft red glow to include that old black tar-papered garage. After dumping another handful of pinecones carefully in the fire pit, he reached over to the table for the newspaper clipping brought to him by that strange woman. As he grabbed it, a smaller clipping fell to the ground. He picked it up and read it. Uncle John read the old paper clipping out loud in a surprised tone, "Toms River New Jersey Courier 10 December 1908—Giberson Mill classroom top honors go to: Ralph Giberson, Willie Webb, Royden Romans, and Daisy Webb." On the last word, Webb, a pinecone popped so loud that Uncle John near fell out of his chair. "Well, I'll be darned."

28

MARSHALL'S CORNER LEGACY

ESTABLISHED 1937–2004

There are two things New Jersey is known for: hotdogs and diners. Jerseyans love their diners, just as much they love hotdogs, whether they come from a cart, truck or diner. This is the story of how the two combined on a busy corner in South Jersey to create an iconic destination. Today, it barely resembles its humble beginnings some one hundred years ago. How does a hot dog stand on a portable cart go on to become a symbol of a community and waypoint for thousands of New Jerseyans heading to the Jersey Shore? With vision and determination to make it in this mean old world, Mr. Lane Marshall Sr. adopted the corner of two busy thoroughfares in the dead center of the state of New Jersey: the town of New Egypt. He was a natural-born salesman who knew that the key to success was to make your own opportunity and feed it well so it could grow. Sadly, they paved paradise and put up a parking lot—literally. Yet that doesn't mean we shouldn't remember its history and revere its place in tens of thousands of family's hearts, right?

Post an image of almost any iconic place in the state, and you'll see people from all walks of life commenting. Even if they visited only once, they formed an attachment to these places. We all naturally have a love for remembering our own experiences as they relate to visiting popular spots. And we are constantly evaluating and reevaluating our own memories of historical events that occur in our lifetimes. Taking the proverbial trip down memory lane is something we all love to do, right?

Marshall's Groceries. *Artist Shane Tomalinas.*

When an image like the one drawn here of Marshall's Corner was posted, the comment thread read like this: "I miss that place! I used to work there." "We used to stop there on the way home from the shore." "My dad and grandfather would stop there after hunting. Was so sad when it went." "That was our lunch place when we were hunting Colliers Mills." "Great little homey restaurant." "They had the best pork cutlet with gravy!" "Was a regular stop." "Marshals Corner to us old timers, and we still call it that. Even though a gas station takes its place." "My mom and dad would go up there occasionally." "When we walked in, we would always look around to see who else was there." "Blast from the past!"

There are hundreds of similar comments from families and friends who remember a place that isn't that far gone in our memories. It had become a staple in the daily lives of locals and thousands of weary travelers looking for a hot or cold drink.

Ironically, Mr. Lane Marshall Sr. moved to the area from New York. The ironic part is the place he built became beloved by both outsiders and locals. Usually, a local watering hole has a vibe all its own. Sometimes, it feels as if it belongs to locals only. It's an interesting and sometimes heated

This page: The store as it appeared in Lane Marshall Sr.'s day, circa the 1950s. *Courtesy of the Marshall family.*

debate when one becomes part of a community. Arguably, it's an endless waste of energy. Some would say it's tiring, too. The argument of "us versus them," or "we're insiders and you're an outsider," exists in our culture to divide—unlike the reality of the situation. Another popular phrase is "Bennies, go home" if you're in the shore region. But within our culture and our communities, the lines blur, as everyday people mingle at a wrap-around counter,

swapping stories over ice-cold sodas or several cups of hot steaming black coffee. After all, America and most towns in New Jersey—our state being one of the most diverse in the country—are big homogeneous melting pots. And they were on the go even before the automobile craze of the 1950s. Towns and cities were built by people who were once outsiders; they established places of cultural significance that became icons of an era. Marshall's Corner, an anonymous source said, was "near as important as the Statue of Liberty on Ellis Island. To people on the move, cross state." Did they overstate its importance? Probably not, for every community needs a gathering place. Sometimes, those places take on lives of their own. One has to wonder if Lane Sr. knew this would be the future for his corner of the world.

Families and friends would come in daily to patronize the establishment before it ultimately succumbed to interstate progress in 2000. Those who lived close by were lucky enough to taste their favorite menu items one last time.

These menu items included:

> *Breakfast served all day the Trifecta Omelet a three egg omelet w/ potatoes toast and jelly and pick your filling $4.35 hit the spot, after a long morning of hunting for lunch the Maxie Burger when you're hungry as a horse $5.59, and the end of the day meal might have been a Crazy Horse Cutlet a 12oz freshly breaded fried pork cutlet & saw horse gravy $7.99.*

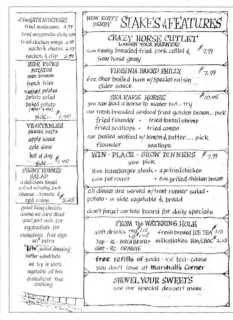

Opposite: The last menu cover for Marshall's Corner Restaurant. *Courtesy of John Blanda.*

This page: Marshall's Corner Restaurant menu. *Courtesy of John Blanda.*

Today, the once-bustling highway pit stop and community gathering place has been erased by progress. Even the grandchildren of the original owner of Marshall's Groceries, who were once under their grandparents' protective wing in and around the store, find their fond memories of the old place are fading. Let's talk to one of the last people who remembers the old days, when people weren't afraid to get out of the fast lane for a tasty burger or an ice-cold milkshake at Marshall's Groceries, which predated the restaurant of recent memory aptly named Marshall's Corner.

Enter Mrs. Rose Marshall (née Blanda, age ninety-five):

> *Jack's father* [Rose's husband], *Lane Matthew Marshall Sr., died in 1959. He was the original owner and founder of Marshall's Groceries there on Lakewood Road and Pinehurst Road. At the time, I ran the store for a year by myself; then my husband, Jack Marshall, took over until we sold it in 1969.*

Jack's father was born in Luftkin, Texas, in 1902. From 1919 to 1923, it was the navy that took the blue-eyed, brown-haired man to the East Coast, New York City in particular. There, he eventually caught the eye of Elsie Corin Richards, a naturalized resident of New York originally from England. They were married in October 1923, and at first, they resided in Brooklyn, New York, and eventually made their way to New Jersey in the 1930s. The 1940 federal census reports Lane Marshall, with his seventh-grade education, was a service station owner and operator who lived with his wife, Elsie Marshall, and their three children, Elsie, Lane and Samuel. By the 1950 federal census, Lane Marshall was the owner and operator of a road stand and service station at the now-established Marshall's Corner in New Egypt, New Jersey.

> *I remember my husband telling me that Elsie and Lane Sr. got their start in 1937 on Pinehurst Road in New Egypt, New Jersey. It started out as a service station, then added a little stand of hotdogs and cold soda along with gas pumps. It wasn't until later that the store was added and then enlarged in 1956. The family lived in a house on Greenwood Avenue in Trenton, where Lane worked for a company called Thermoid. They specialized in brake linings and the tire industry. Tradition says my father-in-law and many other families from the old neighborhood in Brooklyn bought homes in a startup community called Pinehurst Estates, south of where, eventually, Lane Marshall Sr. would build out his future on a tiny corner where the two dirt roads met. Before long, Lane had purchased new property along Lakewood Road and Pinehurst Road of New Egypt, where he located the original hotdog stand that would become known as Marshall's Corner. Eventually, he built a garage with an apartment overhead at the site.*

Lane Marshall Sr. and his wife, Elsie, circa the 1940s. *Courtesy of the Marshall family.*

At the beginning of the twentieth century, when Mr. Lane Marshall Sr. was alive, at pinch points along the railroad, shops and businesses blossomed, with new patrons coming from far away by train. They added to the local economy and supported a cottage industry of away-from-home hospitality, like the Pine Tree Inn in Lakehurst that was a short carriage ride from the railroad tracks. Many from the north spent the winter months here. The Pine Tree Inn provided the idea of summer cottages for city travelers who wanted a piece of paradise without having to stay in an inn or hotel. It was not just a getaway for a few days or a week in the summer, but it was also an escape in the winter months, as it was warmer in South Jersey than it was in New York. Usually, the mothers and children would stay throughout the week in summer, while the men would come back down from the cities by bus for the weekends.

By the 1940s, this railroad-boosted economy showed signs of wear and cracking, as Americans took to the road in the family automobile. The foot and horse trails of Natives that were adopted by early settlers became dirt roads and were happily used at the beginning of the automobile craze. During that time, places like a hot dog and cold soda stop were welcome to weary travelers in the rural countryside. Lane and Elsie catered to the times along that highway of dirt, for it would be years before the highway maintenance improvements were funded. In this period, hawkish real estate speculators pushed land parcels to city folk to start new communities. Eventually, many of these would-be communities failed or waned and were never finished. And many homes and or summer cottages that were located on the new military bases of World War I were cleared to make way for training sites and base housing. As early as 1921, the establishment of Lakehurst Naval Air Station occurred.

Summer places that were on now military land could be moved for the federal government had no use for them. Lane Matthew Marshall Sr. and

191

wife, Elsie, moved at least one, maybe two, of the buildings from where everyone from the Brooklyn neighborhood had summer places at Pinehurst Estates (on Pinehurst Road) halfway to Beckerville (today, all that is left is Beckerville Road) on righthand side. The government got that land, and they had to vacate. And the Marshalls bought the whole corner to Success Lane and to County Route 539, where Baldoff, Pancoast, Tumm property is. They all knew each other back in Brooklyn and it only made sense that they purchased land from my father-in-law, who had plenty of acreage at the new site just north of the old one. Elsie and Lane Sr. lived in a house that burned to the ground just left of Marshall's Groceries. Lane Sr. built onto that house, as it was part of a cottage in Pinehurst community like the main part of the store was. Jack and I had our wedding reception there and lived there for a little while in 1947–48 with Jack's parents. There's a funny story about why Jack was named Jack. My mother-in-law was English, and my father-in-law was an American sailor when she married him. In England, sailors were nicknamed "Jack Tar". Tradition says Lane M. Marshall Jr., my husband, got the nickname "Jack" because of that old carryover from the mother country. He was born on November 8, 1926, in Long Island City to the late Lane Marshall Sr. and Elsie C. Marshall, née Richards.

A side note: Beckersville was once called Yankeetown. When Edward F. Larrabee sold his 174-acre plot to William Becker and the family prospered with a flower farm that supplied the New York flower market, the town became known as Beckersville. It was part of Manchester but became part of Lakehurst Borough in later years. A curious note is that there are no records of the Pinehurst community existing where Elsie and Lane Marshall Sr. moved a building or two north to New Egypt, but there is World War II navy base housing called Pinehurst Estates. This is odd, though there was a town called Beckersville where, today, there remains a road named Beckersville Road. But the navy housing called Pinehurst Estates is nowhere near Pinehurst Road. And there's no record of Pinehurst Estates, but oral history and the people's memory says otherwise.

Clifford "Mickey" Horner III remembered the families who relocated to Marshall's Corner:

The Horner and Enriquez families moved (three there) from same neighborhood in Brooklyn, New York, to the outskirts of the neighborhood of New Egypt, New Jersey. Mr. Fred Nix and Mr. Gowdy were the only other neighbors who owned homes along the road they too purchased land parcels from Mr. Marshall. Clifford Horner Jr. (deceased 2003) and Teresa Lynn Enriquez (my mom's sister) built their houses along the same dirt road.

Entrusting his old neighborhood friend, Mr. Lane Marshall Sr. sold small plots to each of the families. The lots were small in comparison to today's Plumsted Township ordinance for a minimum requirement of five acres. Each family bought a near-acre-sized plot—in some cases just a one-third of an acre—from Mr. Marshall, keeping the families close together. Family members shared hopes of escaping the stresses of city life, even if only for a short time. You could say that the hot dog stand of Mr. Marshall united these families in many ways. First, it made them physical neighbors, and in one case of love, at least two young souls were tied together by a strand of black hair that twirled in the winds generated from shore traffic flying by. Alice "Peggy" Enriquez was the one with the coal-black hair twirling in the wind.

Clifford "Mickey" Horner III continued:

Mr. Marshall hired my mom (Peggy Enriquez) to watch over his little hotdog stand, and in doing so, she got to escape city life for the summer in the 1930s while her boss worked in the city of Trenton. My mom met my dad at that very hot dog stand at Lane Marshall's corner service station, and the two fell in love, with the gal soon to become Mrs. Clifford "Mickey" Horner Jr. Dad was a local boy from Long Swamp Road, and his dad, "Micky" Horner Senior, was born a stone's throw away on Hockamick Road. [Botany and hybridizing blueberry bushes were what Mickey Sr. was known for, and he assisted Enoch Bills in cultivating his blueberry patch on Cranberry Canners Road in New Egypt, New Jersey.] *And now their progeny continues to live in the same town as generations before. Micky IV, and his son the fifth Micky Horner, live in the very same house on Success Road that was built by generations before. Some things change, while other things remain the same. And the family name continues to grow, as a Horner descendant lives within the same four walls. Lane Marshall Sr. and my uncle Tom Enriquez built a log cabin using trees from the land which it was built upon. It still stands today on Success Road, and my uncle used it to vacation on the weekends. Just as the Marshall blood still resides at various places on Success Road today. The only other houses there besides a sand pit and the*

Ms. Elizabeth Tumm, nicknamed "Toodles" by friends, age ninety-one (*left*); and Mrs. Rose Marshall, age ninety-five. *Author's collection.*

remaining part of Success Road that bypasses Marshall's Corner through the woods also connects Route 528 and Route 539. The north end of Success Road is paved today, whereas the southeast end is still dirt. At that end of Pinehurst Road that turns onto Route 539, the Tumms and the Baldoffs lived and still live today.

Enter Ms. Elizabeth Tumm (age ninety-one). She was nicknamed "Toodles" by friends after the popular doll from the 1950s/1960s named Toddles. She was another longtime resident of Marshall's Corner whose original summer cottage is now her full-time home alongside Success and Pinehurst Roads.

My mother's name was Rose, and my father's name was Charles. The earliest information I could find on my family coming here is in this first deed to this property to my home is 1940. The second deed from 1944 is another part of the parcel. Then a third deed later added a small piece of land to the other two, forming our home here. My father bought one piece of land from one neighbor, but the other two originally were bought from Lane Sr. and Elsie Marshall. Upon the property, a two-room cottage, sixteen feet by twelve feet was built by Elsie Marshall's stepfather, Mr. Robert Hellen, at a cost not to exceed $175. A signed contract from both parties in New

York City at the time is evidence of this. Our cottage had no electricity and a pump in the yard for water, including an outhouse for a bathroom. We slept on cots in the one room space. Back then, it was the whole summer house; today, it's the living room part of my house. But back then, in the morning, you picked them up, and the space was used for visiting and such. I can remember Grandpa Bauer listened to a battery-operated radio in one of the corners of the one-room house.

I was born in 1931 and was eight or nine years old here at Marshall's Corner. I imagine my parents were friends with Lane, even back when they owned a cottage in the Pinehurst Estates. When they and Lane Sr., who had already gotten land north of my parents, had to move out of Pinehurst, they purchased the parcels from Lane and contracted for the summer cottage to be built by Robert Hellen (the stepfather of Elsie Marshall). My memories are from the 1930s and 1940s summer vacations until the 1960s, when we moved to Jersey permanently after a second housing space was built here at Marshall's Corner. My mother had two brothers (Frank and John). They picked tomatoes at the Bauer farm and stayed with us, too. My Uncle Frank was great at telling ghost stories, and me and my younger sister Rose (nicknamed "Cookie") would listen intently, and I can remember one time my mother popping her head through a window in the front of the house, and we screamed. He was that good at storytelling.

My father, Charles, worked five days a week as a produce company delivery driver in New York City. On the weekends, we would get in the car and travel down to the cottage—never in the winter, because the cottage was only good for warm weather. When the last day of school in New York came, we were packed and ready to go to Jersey. There were no early outs like today; you went to school all the way to the 30th of June. In the city, with all the cement and tall buildings, it was very hot. When we went to New Jersey, it was a relief. It was so cool there. We spent the summers here along with my parents' younger brother and sisters. We only went to the shore once or twice a year. The lake at Colliers Mills was it. Colliers Mills was everything to us back then. We walked there to go swimming, mostly because my father would go back to New York to work during the week, and he took the family car. Sometimes, he'd ride the bus down to save on gas. During the war, he would get a bus from the Port of Authority of New York to Lakewood, then to here at Marshall's Corner. We went back home after Labor Day to go back to school. I can remember the only people we saw at Colliers Mills were a schoolteacher and his wife with their children from Monmouth Road. They would meet us at Colliers Mills. It was just us.

We all came down; every day, we rode our bikes. I taught all the younger cousins to swim along the beach at the lake. I was the oldest, and I can remember it being great, picking wild blueberries and swimming all day, then riding our bikes back to Marshall's Corner, where you'd rarely see a car on the road. It was safe as can be for us back then.

It was an idyllic setting for both the young and old there at the corner of Pinehurst and Lakewood Roads. It wasn't until a sudden decline in health that Mr. Lane Marshall Sr. let go of the pump and finally stopped peppering the grill with fresh handmade hamburger patties. In 1958, thanks to a long-time employee, the business continued under Betty Hopkins's guidance. Then Lane's daughter-in-law stepped in and ran the place for a year. All alone, Mrs. Rose Marshall handled the books, the service station end and the store operations all at once. In tough and uncertain times, families pull together and get the job done. Mrs. Elsie Marshall could not run the store herself, and most of the children were in California and did not want to be part of the family business, so the family turned to the best solution for all: Lane "Jack" M. Marshall Jr. and his wife, Rose, were thrust into the family business. Jack, like his father, was known for being a good salesman. They say he could "sell ice to an Eskimo." And by taking over the family business, not only did Jack and Rose help support their aging mother Elsie and teenage brother Bill, but they also helped an important icon to the community keep its light on. They helped sustain the extended family Lane Sr. had cultivated from young sprouts. Marshall's Corner grew under their loving hands and so did the place in the hearts of so many locals and travelers down life's highway that ran east and west and north to south to the Jersey Shore. Each owner, Lane and Lane Jr., were probably too busy to realize it, but they were building friendships and meaningful lives for themselves, all while fostering community. They were not just serving food; they were serving people and providing a place for others to have a good time. And that goes for future Marshall generations as well.

Mrs. Rose Marshall continued:

We had people working for us, usually only two local people at a time. Two of the longest store helpers were Betty Hopkins and Pauline Kenner. Betty opened the store in the early morning, for she was the longest-running employee who had worked for Lane Marshall Sr. and ran the place when Lane got sick. Another full-time employee, a local, too, was Pauline Kenner. At the time, I had young children. With Jack and I being the closest thing

A typical uniform of the neighborhood Bond Bread delivery driver in the 1930s. *Leonard Miner; courtesy of the Jersey City Free Library.*

to help take over the family business in 1959, when Lane Marshall Sr. died, that's what we did. At the time, Jack was working for Bond Bread in Trenton in the 1950s, but after a year of going it alone, Jack joined me. He left his job there in Trenton and took over the operations of the store.

The store was named Marshall's Groceries, and the original building material came from Pinehurst Estates. It was a simple setup at the start, and in later years, it had a full kitchen and dining room and was aptly renamed Marshall's Corner. In that ten-year period, Rose and her husband, Jack, kept the menu pretty much the same as it had been back in Lane Marshall Sr.'s day. Lane had sold Seiler pork roll since 1938, and they continued selling this pork roll in the 1950s. Rose recounted one of the only technology upgrades. "When I was at the house, I'd get a Bell telephone call asking to flip the record. Back then, we had a wire speaker running from our house, where the record player with the stack of records was playing out to the store, and I'd be raising our young children at home and would hang up the phone and flip the stack of records or put on new ones when it would run out." In later years, they got a jukebox that sat in the grocery section of the store next to the pinball machine. But neither generation of owners of Marshall's Groceries needed to debate whether it was Taylor Ham or pork roll, for they

GAISER'S RESTAURANT
Lakewood Rd. New Egypt
Now Serving Steaks to Pancakes

Mon - Thurs 6:30 a.m. to 8:00 p.m.
Fri & Sat 6:30 a.m. to 10:00 p.m.
Sunday 8:00 a.m. to 10:00 p.m.

NIGHTLY SPECIALS

Wed. - Spaghetti & Meatballs	$2.75
Thurs. - Club Steak	$3.75
Fri. - Fresh Fish & Chips	$2.95
Steamed Clams doz.	$2.85

LUNCH TIME SPECIALS

Hot Roast Beef on Hard Roll - with Cole Slaw &
French Fries $1.95

Rueben Sandwich with Potatoe Salad & Cole Slaw
                                                $1.95

COOKED DAILY

Compliments
of
of

The Seilers
CHRISTIAN F. SEILER
JULIUS F. SEILER
WILLIAM G. SEILER
ALBERT H. SEILER

JOS. SEILER SONS CO.

Mfg. of
Trenton's Finest Meat Products

Left: Gaiser's Restaurant advertisement in the *New Egypt Press*, July 20, 1978. *Author's collection.*

Above: The Seilers, Trenton's Finest Meat Products, card, circa the 1950s. *Author's collection.*

purchased the best pork roll straight from German butchers and the owners of Manufacturers of Trenton's Finest Meat Products, Joseph Seiler Sons Company. The store had a long Formica counter for sandwiches, coffee and ice cream. It was just a counter in front of stools, nothing fancy. It didn't become a fully functioning restaurant until James Gaiser purchased it in 1969, changing its name to Gaiser's, but after it was sold to the last owner, John Barulic, it became known as Marshall's Corner (1984–2004). This was done with the blessing of Rose and Jack Marshall with the condition that it continued the restaurant tradition.

In our ten-year run, we kept the operation the same as Lane Matthew Marshall Sr. My husband even kept the same box of unpaid credit lines as far back as Lane Marshall Sr., always doing our best to help others in need. It wasn't easy on us either. I can remember the store's layout. You walked in the front door, we had groceries for sale, like canned goods, cereal, cigarettes and candy. Mostly, our customers were people that went to the shore. We had gas pumps out front selling Mobil gas, Lakewood Oil Company providing oil for the cars and kerosene for customers' heating needs. But we also had bread, milk and cold cuts and the grill, so local people came, too. Potted meat was an item the local migrant workers would come in and buy from us. I guess lunch was mostly our main attraction and the milkshakes we made. One of the regulars the Marshalls' children knew as Papa Joe. Joseph Emery helped pump gas when an extra hand was needed. When

This page: Marshall's Corner Restaurant, February 2002. *Courtesy of Elizabeth Tumm.*

we had the store, he was retired and enjoyed being in the shop, a nice local guy who drank coffee along with a group of locals who socialized at the wrap-around counter. We never paid him to lend a hand, he just did. Oh, we built onto the business a garage and started selling tires out of the basement. [Marshall's Corner Tire Company was located on Lakewood Road in New Egypt, New Jersey 08533. It was a Goodyear Tire certified dealer.]

But we continued the tradition of using the same local merchants for our supplies and the same delivery guys who provided our store's staples. Whether purchasing our pork roll from Seiler, locally sourced fresh farm eggs from Robson's farm, bread from Freihofer's Bakery, customer favorite Lehigh Valley scoop ice cream or the brewing of Maxwell House coffee that Papa Joe and everyone else enjoyed, we still prepared

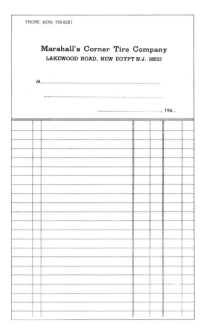

Marshall's Corner Tire Company, 1960s invoice. *Courtesy of the Marshall family.*

and cooked our homemade recipe for burgers sourced from the Main Street butcher Ralph Cliff. Along with precuring our large collection of candy, cigarettes and cigars from Trenton tobacco company, things remained the same. And do you know, in all those ten years, we were only able to take one vacation? At the time, our oldest daughter, Lorraine "Cookie" Hilburn, née Marshall (1948–1998), watched the stand while Jack and I went on vacation for a few days to Montreal, Canada, in 1967. First and last time, because even though we owned a business, it wasn't making anyone wealthy or rich, and each of us had to work long hours, and were tied to the store.

Papa Joe from Hawkins Road died in 1986, but if he was alive when the place turned the last page of its life to become Marshall's Corner Restaurant, he probably would have sat at the new counter and ordered coffee from the new owners. Doing something as simple as buying a cup of coffee at a place that reminds you of yesterday—when you were younger and the world was different—helps us all find peace. It's different—not better, just different. Around the world, lives are lived at the end of a Formica counter over a cup

Marshall's Corner regulars sitting at the counter on Good Friday, April 13, 2001. Howard Powell is wearing a hat and sitting with Frank Dye. *Author's collection.*

Marshall's Corner regulars Lisa Marcigliano and, in the foreground, Richard Emery sitting at the counter on Good Friday, April 13, 2001. *Author's collection.*

Kristina Lewis, a waitress, in uniform in the dining area of Marshall's Corner in 2001. *Author's collection.*

Left to right: Debbie Young and Helene Kaveski waiting on Marshall's Corner customers at the counter in 2001. *Author's collection.*

of coffee and the shared community of others. The grocery section of the store sold select goods until the end, when the bulldozers came knocking. From the late 1990s, the pressure of a convenience store built across the highway meant the once vital grocery shop of must-have perishable home goods (milk, bread and cereal) and potted meats was no longer needed, and John and Liz Baurlic added an antique/curio shop for patrons of the restaurant. Was the concept of a sit-down community diner on that corner also antiquated? And did the competition across the street spell doom for the once thriving corner store?

You hear locals whisper, "Don't tell anyone how great we got it here, or they'll all come here and ruin it for us!" The thing is, a town's character changes every few centuries under the umbrella of progress. And you can't keep the outside at bay, because some of the places you love have a life of their own and become destinations for passersby and tourists alike. At the counter and, later, at a table in the bustling restaurant, people made connections with total strangers, some becoming lifelong friends, all from entering Marshall's Corner for reprieve from the busy life on the highway. Inside, time slows down, and the coffee flows, fueling storytelling and laughter. Like the descendants of Lane Marshall Sr., time ticks furiously forward, not backward. If you've witnessed the footprints of generations of New Jerseyans on both sides of the counter, leaving behind bits and pieces of themselves in a gathering place such as Marshall's Corner, you'd have to wonder: "The DNA in the place is like the great melting pot of the people of America, mixed and mingled together, becoming one. Do the Marshall descendants or the community members who patronized the place metaphorically own the deed to one of our state's most revered corners—Marshall's Corner?" We know the land was sold and the deed was turned over to the passage of time and progress, thus lost and paved out of existence.

The landscape changed in the New Egypt community; the highway name became more locally recognized as County Route 539 instead of Pinehurst Road. That road was one of the mainstay routes from the big city of Trenton to the Jersey Shore. That two-lane highway went from being dirt when Lane Sr. owned and operated Marshall's Groceries to being paved in later years, when Marshall's Corner stood steadfast with its dirt parking lot. The paving of the highway and, in the end, the paving of the Marshall's Corner parking lot, led to the buildings of old being torn down, erasing all traces of the original landscape. Icons and historic places fall out of fashion and disappear, while other faces and places of our collective society endure. When they do disappear, all we are left with are memories. Like a parent who's passed away, the stories, physical images and stones we erect in their memory become sacred. The Statue of Liberty, standing for life, liberty and the pursuit of happiness, is a place we can still go to, making the memories of our first visit to the Statue of Liberty not as important as those of a family member who's passed and is gone from this world. For you can still visit and see it again. Memories with all the patched-together details of past occurrences are all we have to keep love alive, making those memories and stories even more precious. Maybe we should respect both before the new pavement cools in the parking lot of progress and the memory begins to fade, lost to time for those who lived it.

We dedicate this story to those who lived it: Lane Matthew Marshall Sr. (1902–1959); his wife, Elsie Marshall (née Richards, 1904–1993); Lane Matthew Marshall Jr., also known as "Jack" (1926–2022); his wife, Rose Marshall (née Blanda, born 1927); Charles Tumm (1910–2000); his wife, Rose Tumm (née Bauer, 1912–2003); Clifford Horner Jr. (1927–2003); and his wife, Peggy Horner (née Enriquez, 1929–2022). These lovely couples' love blossomed and grew into families at Marshall's Corner. We also dedicate this story to the customers who fondly remember Marshall's Corner—some were wee babies at the time, whereas others returned again and again with

SWEET ENDINGS
MARSHALL'S CORNER
EST.1937 - 2004
NEW EGYPT, NJ
ROCKY ROAD CAKE $1¹² a slice
*buy a whole cake... $6⁵⁰
APPLE SPICE PUDDING CAKE. $150
CHEESE CAKE.. $1⁹⁰   *$6⁵⁰
RICE PUDDING... $1⁰⁰
soft
ICE CREAM
cup... $1³⁵
cone sm. $1⁰⁰
LG. $1²⁵
Vanilla
Chocolate
or
twist
Ice cream
SUNDAES
strawberry
chocolate
butterscotch
one big size
$2⁵⁰

The last promotional piece at the restaurant. *Courtesy of Elizabeth Tumm.*

their own babies. Thank you for being part of the community. Remember to always cherish time spent among friends, even though it seems things go on forever and that they'll last longer than life itself—but sometimes, they do sadly end. Farewell, Marshall's Corner of old. On cold nights, they say a random bus from the New Jersey Department of Transportation still stops at the once-bustling bus route stop.

29

DREAMING OF BYGONE DAYS

W here the hell did you come from, boy? You done snuck up on me awfully quick."

An old man sitting on an orange milk crate with a black fishing pole in his hand stood up along the banks of the Rancocas Creek. The boy—he was not really a boy, as he was in his late forties—had just stepped out of a time portal. The old man didn't mean any harm by his tone; he was just being good ole Joe Lewis. He was a country boy down to his boots and green suspenders, tying his fashionable old wispy self together and smartly keeping his blue dungarees from falling. "Well, don't just stand there gawking at me. I've got snappin' turtles to catch. There's an extra chair in the back of the pickup. Help yourself. And the name's Roy."

Perplexed and astounded, the man from the future remained standing. It worked as the salesman said it would. Back in the future, he had stood at the time portal after paying a hefty service fee to a startup company called Bygone Days. Via voice command, the middle-aged man named Billy asked, "I'd like to visit my late paternal grandfather, Joseph Roy Lewis. Please take me to him five years before he died." He thought long and hard about who he'd like to visit and when. He had many fond memories of days spent with his grandparents growing up in southern New Jersey. At home, his mom kept a close watch on him, many said from her fear of losing another child. Her youngest son had died at five months old in 1975 from spinal meningitis. This made her leery and overly watchful of her eldest son, Billy. In all his life, he had never broken a bone in his body—she made sure of that. But

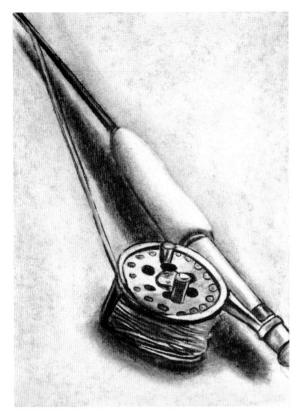

Left: Rod and Reel. *Artist, Shane Tomalinas.*

Below: Amber cedar water in Burlington County. *Author's collection.*

to a young boy, climbing a tree or running through the woods, chasing a cousin in Browns Mills, was all you could want. You can do anything you want at the Lewis house on Junction Road. That's what grandparents are for, after all. They provide the freedom to explore and do the things a loving mother would frown upon. Much of his time was spent out in the Pines with Grandpa along a creek or an old bridge that served as a fishing hole. It wasn't a surprise when Billy found Grandpa along the creek with a pole in one hand and an Old Milwaukee beer in the other.

Those were the days. Late in the afternoon, they'd load the beat-up old pickup with crates for chairs, a couple of pounds of smelly bait from Acme (you don't want to know what the mystery meat was) and a few old fishing poles that were also used down the shore for flounder fishing. They used the kind of fishing poles that had big reels and a spool of a hefty greenish line that held a hook and sinker. These were not the fancy, clear plastic, high-test fishing string used for pickerel fishing, but they were the kind that wouldn't get shredded if they became tangled in a waterlogged stump at the bottom of the creek. It just so happens, snapping turtles lay there, and hopefully, they would fall for the putrid meat bait. The fishing line also had to be strong enough to reel in the heavy turtles from the melancholy cedar waters, especially when those ancient beasts put up a fight and became determined to drag the person on the other end of the line down to their level at the bottom of the creek or pond. The prize, once reeled in from the dark depths of water, made mighty fine fried snapper meat and homemade snapper soup. The time spent along any of the fishing holes with a grandparent meant the world to grandkids—a delicious dinner later was just a happy coincidence.

Coincidently, this is where, in the dream, the artificial intelligence from the startup company Bygone Days took Billy. He grabbed a metal crate from the truck bed. "I guess, Roy, you were too hooked on catching something good that you didn't notice me come down the road there. My name's Billy." He reached a hand out for a shake.

"Well, have a seat quickly; you're gonna scare off the fish. Don't mind me if I refuse your handshake, for we don't do that much around these parts and my hands smell like good snappin' turtle bait and chewing tobacco." Fixing his sweat-stained green hat, the old man went on, "Funny. I got a grandson named Billy. Usually, I can't keep that kid out of the truck when he's around. I tease him with the nickname I gave him, 'Pumper Will.' A good boy like his dad, Punk."

Turtles in the creek. *Author's collection.*

Playing along, future Billy said, "You got colorful names for folks around here. Pumper Will and Punk—I thought being called Billy by my folks was funny."

"They called me Roy since I was a little one, and my big brother is called Lot. Now, those aren't made-up names; they are our birth-given middle names. Of course, if you were to show them to me on a piece of paper, I couldn't tell you which was which, for I don't have much need for that business."

It wasn't a cheap service to contract with Bygone Days, so Billy had spent a lot of time preparing for this conversation and had plenty of questions, but he didn't want to spoil the chance to just be with Grandpa Lewis again either. So, he tempered his excitement and mind full of questions and asked only choice questions. "The business of reading and writing? How come?"

After tossing an empty can into a bucket and grabbing another from an old green metal army cooler with the initials "U.S." on the side, Roy responded, "Grandad and my dad both were dirt farmers from the Pemberton area. Me, I got a backyard plot that we get our vegetables from, but I'm no farmer. I rather not be tied to one piece of land. For one thing, the land isn't cheap. For another, these Pines beg you to get out in 'em. And there's a whole lot of 'em, too. No time sitting down—I'd rather be out pulling grapevine bails or cutting hoghuck. Better yet, I'd rather be junkin', but there's very little money in that. Still, I do it all the time, as you see on TV those guys named Fred Sandford and Lamont. They're funny. None of that needs a college degree. Growing up on a farm, no one was there, inspiring you to go to school when you and your hands were more needed on the farm than in school, learning. And when I'm not doing any of that to put food on the table, I'm out here in the Pines, enjoying the quiet while working to put a different kind of food on the table. You can't find nothing better tasting than my Marie's fried snapper. And if the kids don't finish off the iced tea before dinner that she makes homemade in the sun, well, you got all that is needed in life—a good wife, a full belly and little ones to keep the family going. Speaking of supper, looks like the sun's going down. Best wrap this up and get."

The man from the future looked like he wanted to cry. The one stipulation or catch to the service provided by Bygone Days was that you couldn't leave the area the door opened to. The AI system searched through the vast catalogue of humans to find the person's name requested and queried the timeframe from the requestor before creating the split in the field of time, thus opening the door to the past. That split or doorway was tied to the human of the past but limited by their presence and their presence only. You could stay there for as long as you wanted, visiting only that person. It lasted only as long as the person from the past was there and expired when they departed. Once they left, the thirty-foot diameter of the door the requestor/ time traveler was sent back to the future. That meant once Grandpa left, within less than three car lengths, the visit would be over.

"Roy, do you know what year it is?" Roy finished reeling in the sinker and hook. Fiddling with the bait to remove it from the hook, he replied, "Don't be dumb. It's 1982. You ain't trying to call me stupid, are you? 'Cause I might not be book smart, but I'm no dummy."

Billy jokingly said, "No, no. I meant no offense. I just couldn't think of it myself."

Roy's eyebrows shot high on his stubbled face as he smiled and said, "You remind me a bit of my Marie's first two children. They had a weird sense of humor, those two. Died too young Wayne and Sarah did."

"What do you mean by Marie's first two children, Roy?"

Roy answered, "My kids, too, just not by blood. They were Brittons—those Brittons have a funny sense of humor." He loaded the fishing equipment and crates into the truck.

"One more question before you leave, Roy. I do appreciate your hospitality and talking to me. It sounds like you adopted two kids. Did you ever have any kids of your own?"

Dreaming on pillows of clouds. *Author's collection.*

"I don't much talk about family matters, as there's not much to say. Sure, my Marie; that's Sarah's middle name, like how I go by my birth-given middle name, Roy. When Marie came along, she had those two; then we had four kids ourselves. It ain't hard raising kids. It's a lot like farming corn. There you are, looking down the row, when each seed sprouts. You do what you can to keep the weeds out, to keep the soil watered and fertilized, giving them a chance to grow. Some of the sprouts take off with not much care from you at all, and others need extra help along the way. Come to think of it, there's a lot of work involved in raising little ones—too much like farming for my likes, to tell the truth of it. That's why the grandkids are so much fun. Take Billy, for instance. He doesn't need anything from me but to be told there's room back at the house for him to sleep over and that we're going fishing later. That boy's blond hair and blue-eyed smile are contagious. It's why I call him Pumper Will, for he's gonna have it easy with the women folk someday. You take care, boy." He then got in the truck and started to drive away with a wave.

Waving back, Billy from the future cried out as that familiar beat-up pickup from a memory long ago drove away, "Not sure if it was 'easy' getting a gal, Grandpa, but I got one as good as your Marie!" A time portal appeared, and an alarm rang in this author's bedroom.

30

TALE OF TWO BRIDGES

A casual conversation with your folks stirs emotions and memories you misplaced for decades. It goes something like, "Do you remember when?" And commentary comes about the taste of catfish today versus the taste of fish you caught fresh out of the creeks in the neighborhood. It has you doubling down on those feelings of loss—at least if you grew up in rural America, where the landscape has changed year after year and, sometimes, season after season. Wouldn't it be nice if nothing ever changed and the viewpoint we had as children remained the same, ever curious with something to explore around every corner? Back then, if you were asked the same question, your view might be different. Most of us wouldn't agree with the future version of ourselves. Fond memories often leave out the tough times our families lived through. Yet we love to walk down memory lane, even if for just a little while.

There are two bridges in my own life that physically and metaphorically transport me back to those bygone days. Each has a story attached to them. Do they warrant a retelling here? Appease me a little and think back to when you yourself were little and things seemed different than they are today. There's a song that sings, "life is a highway," which is just dandy. If you've driven on a New Jersey three-lane highway, the speed alone scares the hell out of you, lending truth to the notion that life is a highway, going in all directions at various speeds. Isn't that just plain dandy? What if, while you're cruising down the highway, passing green numbered exit signs, you see, at one of them, a truck entering the highway going the wrong way,

Left: Historic Walnford. *Artist, Charlotte Lewis (née Emery).*

Below: An old iron bridge near Historic Walnford, April 2021. *Author's collection.*

aiming directly toward you? Some would say, "My life flashed before my eyes!" Right before you change lanes to dodge the fool, speeding toward you is the concrete median. Metaphorically speaking, the same sort of collision occurs in the days of our youth—the illegally driven car destined for collision is what society calls progress, and you and I are in the fast lane, minding our own businesses, not knowing things can and will change in the blink of an eye.

Two iron bridges span ancient waterways. Over the years, with man's need to prosper and succeed, each has been repaired and replaced. For progress to succeed, it must continue forward and over bridges, highways, lifetimes and time immemorial. But it's what is under the bridges that conjures up those fond memories. In the north, near a place called Walnford, is a bridge that the local people simply call the Iron Bridge. Under said bridge, the waters flowed in a northwestern direction, where eventually, Crosswicks Creek empties out into the Delaware River. It's a waterway that wraps loosely around the capital of New Jersey, the city of Trenton. It's in the body of water under the rusty, old iron bridge that the memory clings, dripping with love of a simpler time and a simple pleasure. The pleasure was of a young boy fishing with his grandfather. And in those dark waters were some of the tastiest catfish known to the land. And on occasion, a frightening snake-like fish commonly known as an eel could be caught, too. Today, you rarely—if ever—see someone sitting along the banks of Crosswicks Creek, fishing for the bottom-feeding catfish. If you polled your friends who have children today, I bet many would say they never fished with their grandfather, especially under an old iron bridge in the Crosswicks Creek (which our nation's first president certainly dipped his toes in while traversing the area during the American Revolution). Crosswicks Village has plenty of connections to the American Revolution, and at least one residence still has a rusty iron cannonball lodged in it.

Another iron bridge in southern New Jersey harkens to olden times as well. Many explorers of today use it to escape to the sparsely populated Pine Barrens National Reserve. Locals affectionately call the old roadways and highways that crisscross southern parts of the state sugar sand roads. Ghosts and ghost towns both linger on the landscape, as do cherished memories of old for the blessed few who grew up in the Pines. Today, people visit the Pine Barrens region on foot, on the water, by bike and or in the car, all looking to explore the unknown and lose the headaches of home. It feels more remote than it is—maybe because GPS and cellphone coverage is sparse here, as are other modern-day conveniences like Walmarts or gas stations. The local people called Pineys have been all but forgotten by the state. This is as they

The Green Bank Bridge, pictured, is just a four-mile drive northeast of Lower Bank Bridge. *Author's collection.*

A fresh-cut pineycraft cattail bundle. *Author's collection.*

A meadow of cattails. *Author's collection.*

wish it to be, but many can fondly recall the plains of Warren Grove dotted with Piney figures pulling pinecones on sandy hillsides off Route 539 or farther south, where the other iron bridge resides. It's a memory of what once was, when Piney families would be spread out as far as the eye can see under Lower Bank Bridge (and, on occasion, Green Bank Bridge) and alongside the banks of the Mullica River in the cattail meadows to harvest brown-stalked cattails for the dried flower industry. Those waters also served our first president's men during the American Revolution. Pirating and privateering went hand in hand here, stretching across the high seas to the calm waters of the Mullica River and other inland rivers that touch the bay.

Today, they are but passing memories of what once was. They happily take us down memory lane, to a time when things seemed simpler. Life was less busy. Surely, there is a bridge or two—physical and or metaphorical—in each of our past lives that can be found to take us to those wonderful places of yesterday and yesteryear. These are the places where our traditions and culture were formed around the nucleus of the family and are typical for many of us who grew up in New Jersey's vast countryside. They contrast so well with the urban fortresses that spread across the state from the north to the south. City life is painted on one side of the canvas or bridge, and rural life is painted on the other. Neither is good or bad—they are just different. Man's iron rusts along with faded memories. We polish them up occasionally so as to not lose them forever. Thank you for journeying with us as we cruised along memory lane.

Opposite: A wasp with a pinecone for a stinger, the Piney Tribe logo. *Artist, Taylor Harpster.*

PINEBALLS

An Easter egg in media is something that's hidden inside of said media. Wikipedia states, "An Easter egg is a message, image, or feature hidden in software, a video game, a film, or another—usually electronic—medium." The list below is symbolic of hidden messaging or symbolism throughout this text. They do not quite meet the definition of an Easter egg, so we will call them pineballs. Traditional folklore passed from one person to another through oral storytelling is filled with symbolism. As the author, I would like to reveal some of the secret meanings, or pineballs, that connect to the various parts of the stories contained within.

i.   Unceremoniously, the name Jersey Devil is found printed eighteen times (nineteen, if you count this mention) in this book.

ii. The black and white photograph of the house on route 206 on the cover, by no other than Jennifer Andzeski, also known as Primitive Piney on social media, differs from the artist rendition in the chapter. A rocking chair was intentionally drawn into the real-life setting of the house on 206 in Southampton, New Jersey. At no time was there ever a rocking chair out in front of the home. This is the artist Tomalinas's rendition, which replaces the sofa armchair with a rocker that dovetails with the storyline.

iii. Only one out of the thirty original artworks contained within this book was contributed by Charlotte Lewis. She was the mother of author William J. Lewis and the grandmother of artist Mr. Shane Tomalinas. Her artwork can be seen today in a public outdoor setting. The painting *Historic Walnford* appeared in print in October 2012 on a national park–like sign in Plumsted Township along the Crosswicks Creek at Volunteer Park, Evergreen Road, New Egypt, New Jersey.

iv. This book in its entirety is as prickly as a pineball. At the end of 2022, the plan was to hire an editor to begin a book project that involved short motivational stories. This editor had to quit the project due to an overwhelming workload; they were followed by a second editor who quit after a few months, ending the project in May 2023. In June, a new direction came from forces unknown and brought the collection of thirty stories together. Ultimately, the energies came to fruition in book four for this author.

v. In real life and the story "Marshall's Groceries Legacy: Established 1937–2004," "Papa Joe," or Joseph Emery, died in 1986. There are two images that were taken on Good Friday 2001 that feature the regulars sitting at the counter of Marshall's Corner restaurant. These were taken during the years of the last owner, John Barulic. One of the patrons of the restaurant was Richard Emery, Joseph Emery's second-oldest son out of six children. Papa Joe was the first in the family to be a customer, just as Lane Marshall Sr. was the first to establish the business. Yet both Papa Joe and Lane's children, grandchildren and great-grandchildren sat, worked and played in the same space—separated only by time.

vi. A friend, writer and reporter for the monthly *Beverly Bee*, Dennis Rogers gave this author a music CD of Jim Murphy and the Pine Barons after the story was written. After listening to the song "Lenni-Lenape" once, twice, three times, the story "Tom the Turkey and Theresa the Turtle" expanded and took a more meaningful direction.

vii. The image of a candle holder on a stack of two books has a hidden message. The binding of one book reads, "Ye Olde Book of Lore." This was the suggested title of this book prior to editing and the final title decision.

viii. The photograph of a railroad track in the Pines also appears in the independent ninety-minute documentary film *The Reluctant Piney*, which was based on Arcadia Publishing's 2021 book *New Jersey's Lost Culture*. It's available for free viewing on the YouTube channel Piney Tribe.

ix. In the acknowledgements section of this book, the author mentions a Facebook group called Piney Tribe. The image at the beginning of this Easter egg list is part of the logo of that Pine Barrens–loving community. This is not to be mistaken for the state bird the mosquito but a wasp with a pinecone for a stinger. It's symbolic of the group, which consists of like-minded individuals who believe in the phrase "live and let live." But once provoked, look out for their wrath; they're like the wasp who flies by but, once swung at, will deliver a painful sting 99 percent of the time. You can see this wasp logo printed on bumper stickers adorning vehicles throughout South Jersey. There is even a billboard with the Piney Tribe logo standing twelve feet tall just past four-mile circle southeast on Route 72 in southern New Jersey.

x. If you visit the website Pineytribe.com, you will find a map that lists the thirty locations in southern New Jersey that inspired each of the thirty stories contained in this book. In some cases, they literally take place at the locations on the map. In other stories, the plot itself is shaped by the writer in the coffee shop or place of business. You, too, can visit these locations—if you dare.

xi. Subconsciously but not intentionally, there are only thirteen endnotes. Over the last few centuries, the number thirteen has been labeled as unlucky and a sign of the devil. It adds something of clandestine spookiness to this collection.

NOTES

1. This story, in part, first appeared in *SoJourn* (Summer 2023), published by the South Jersey Culture and History Center at Stockton University.
2. This old nineteenth-century farmhouse, once a home for many fathers, daughters, mothers and so on, was torn down on January 11, 2022. What once was is no more. The house fell to the weathering of time on what was once a prosperous dairy farm in Southampton, New Jersey.
3. Quoted from the New Egypt Flea Market website: "New Egypt Village & Auction was founded by Esler and Sandy Heller in 1959. Open Wednesday & Sunday, Rain or Shine! 933 Monmouth Road New Egypt, NJ 08533."
4. From Howlingwoodsfarm.com: "Howling Woods Farms is a non-profit 501(c)(3) wolf educational center, and we welcome your donations."
5. Without the ecowarriors of South Jersey, there wouldn't be a Forked River Mountains Wilderness Area. People like Elizabeth Morgan, along with the Forked River Mountain Coalition, the Nature Conservancy and Ocean County, helped preserve the two mounts: west 184 feet and east 176 feet. And we must not forget the Native people who came before, who are represented in this tall tale by Tom the turkey and Theresa the turtle of the Lenni Lenape (Delaware tribe). Turkey (Unalachtigo) and Turtle (Unami), respectively. This story was partially inspired by the song titled "Lenni-Lenape" on the 2005 album *Go New Jersey* by Jim Murphy and the Pine Barons.
6. The Great Bay Boulevard Wildlife Management Area, also known as Seven Bridges, in Tuckerton New Jersey (https://www.loc.gov/item/2017881738/).

7. Not to be confused with the Hanover, Pennsylvania eighteenth-century site called Mary Ann Forge and Furnace, where cannonballs were made for George Washington's army. The following is a link to more information on the Browns Mills site, Mary Ann Forge or Marian Forge with its two hammers: https://forums.njpinebarrens.com/threads/mary-ann-forge.6335/.

8. "Ellis was a fiddler, back in 1889, serving as one-third of the Brindle Town orchestra from 1889 to 1897." This quote is from Henry Charlton Beck's 1936 book *Forgotten Towns of Southern New Jersey*, published by E.P. Dutton and Company.

9. Ellis Parker was a well-known detective when Henry Charlton Beck interviewed him for the chapter on Brindle Town in his book *Forgotten Towns*. But later, Ellis Parker became involved in the most famous missing child case of the century, the Charles Lindbergh baby kidnapping. He was later convicted of coercing a false confession from an innocent suspect and sentenced to six years of federal jail time.

10. A young fern before it unfurls its fronds (coiled) is called a fiddlehead. But only one species is eaten in the United States: the fiddlehead of an ostrich fern, or *Matteuccia struthiopteris*. One should learn how to identify and responsibly harvest edible ferns.

11. At the top of Bear Swamp Hill in 2021, a memorial plaque was erected in honor of Major William F. Dimas, an F-105B Thunderchief pilot who died after his plane hit the Bear Swamp Hill fire tower in 1971.

12. Rancocas Creek twists along a historic corridor from Browns Mills west to the Delaware River in Burlington, New Jersey. A grassroots effort to nominate and secure the title for the Rancocas Creek of Burlington County as a National Water Trail was underway as of 2023.

13. This story is reproduced from the bestselling book *New Jersey's Lost Piney Culture*, published by Arcadia Publishing in 2021 and written by William J. Lewis.

ABOUT THE AUTHOR

William J. Lewis is a lifetime resident of the New Jersey Pine Barrens, as were multiple generations of his family before him. He is the author of *New Jersey's Lost Piney Culture* (The History Press, 2021) and *Adventure with Piney Joe: Exploring the New Jersey Pine Barrens* (South Jersey Culture and History Center, 2022). He shares his Piney adventures on social media networks under the name "Piney Tribe." He preaches exploration without exploitation and teaches our children to be tomorrow's environmental stewards. After proudly serving as a U.S. marine, William went on to graduate from Rider University; he founded an environmental nonprofit to get kids outdoors and has served in leadership roles for both government and New Jersey nonprofit organizations.